CHESTER

A PHOTOGRAPHIC GLIMPSE

By
Felicity McCullough

Series: Places to Visit

My Lap Shop Publishers

Plymouth, England

www.mylapshop.com

Copyright

[Copyright 2014 My Lap Shop Publishers](#)

All rights reserved.

No part of this publication may be reproduced, stored in a retrieval system, or transmitted in any form or by any means, electronic, mechanical, photocopying, recording, scanning, or otherwise, without the prior written permission of the Publisher. Requests to the Publisher for permission should be addressed to:

[My Lap Shop Publishers](#),
91 Mayflower Street, Unit 222, Plymouth, Devon PL1 1SB UK

Published by:

[My Lap Shop Publishers](#)
91 Mayflower Street, Unit 222,
Plymouth, Devon, PL1 1SB
United Kingdom
Tel: +44 (0)871 560 5297
[www.mylapshop.com](#)
[About My Lap Shop Publishers](#)

First Edition March 2014

Paperback

ISBN: 978-1-78165-070-7

Introduction to this Photographic Glimpse of Chester

In 2014, for the first time, I visited the City of Chester. I stayed at the Mill Hotel and Spa, which was in walking distance of the City Centre and sights and situated adjacent to the Shropshire Union Canal's main line.

The weather was pleasant and mostly dry, enabling me to take over 1,500 photographs in and around the City.

It has a fascinating history that I hope I have reflected in this visual record of the sights in and around Chester in 2014. The Romans came, Hugh Lupus, a Norman became the first Earl of Chester, battles were fought, destruction occurred and the city was rebuilt and restored. Modern day use has been found for many of the old buildings. Of note, is the city's architecture with more black and white building that I recall seeing anywhere else and have enjoyed documenting some of these buildings photographically.

Chester held many fascinations for me and gave me my first trip on a canal barge. The boat trip up the River Dee was enjoyed all the more for the sunshine and commentary history of the river. The open-top bus tour allowed me to see those places my tired feet couldn't take me and the freshness of an early morning rain shower, gave me many people-free images.

I hope that you enjoy what you see. I have tried to describe what I saw as accurately as possible for your enjoyment.

I recommend highly a visit to Chester, as there was much more I could have seen, explored and taken photographs of.

Felicity McCullough

Chester A Photographic Glimpse

Mill Hotel & Spa Barge

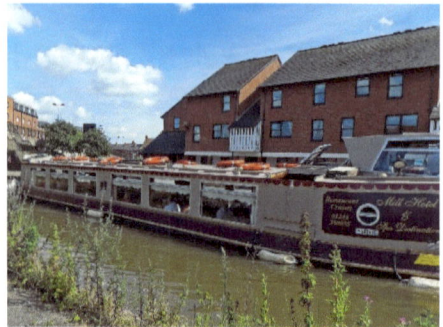

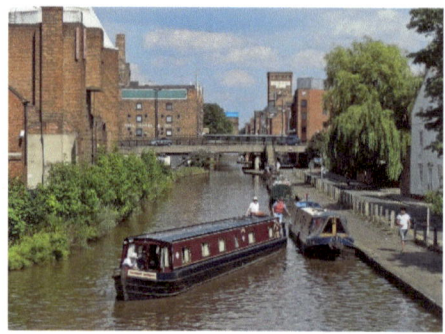

Shropshire Union Canal Main Line, Chester

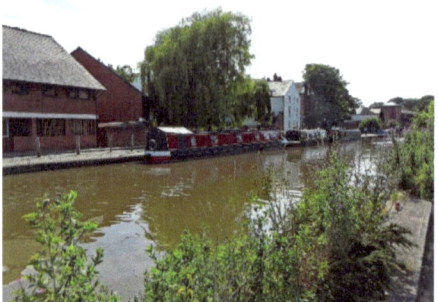

Shropshire Union Canal, Chester

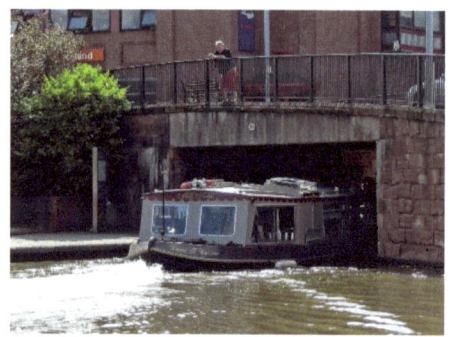

Frodsham Street Bridge over Shropshire Union Canal

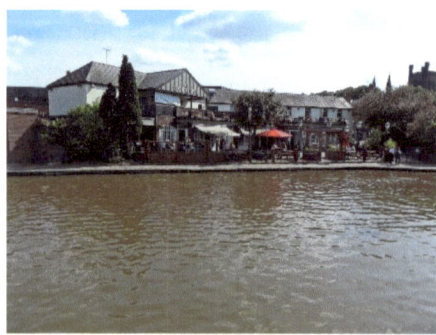

The Gate Keeper Inn, Chester

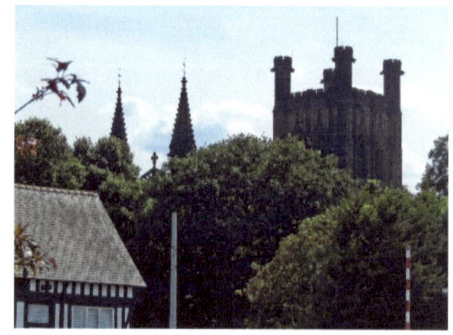

Chester Cathedral Tower and Turrets

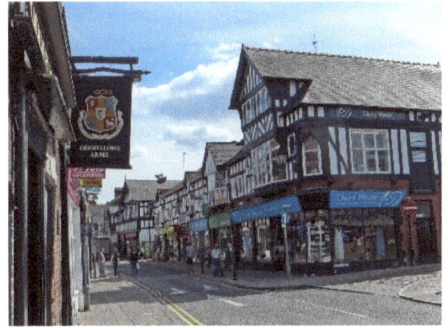

**Frodsham Street, Chester
Black and White Buildings**

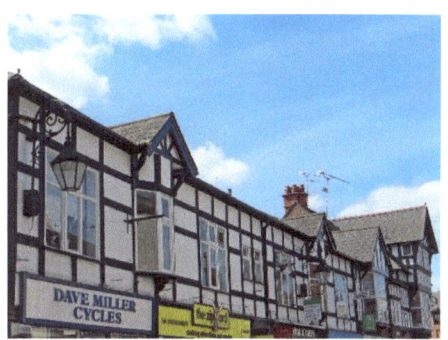

**Frodsham Street, Chester
Black and White Revival
Architecture**

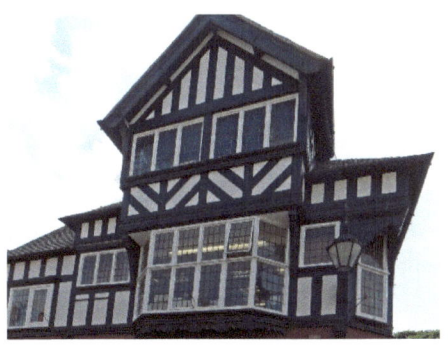

**Frodsham Street, Chester
Black and White Revival
Architecture**

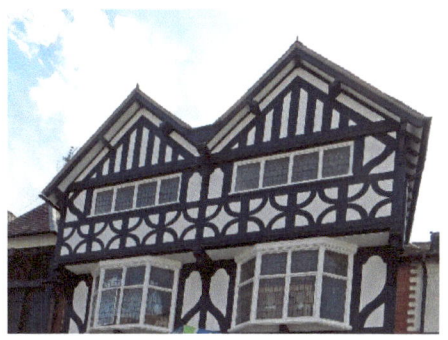

**Frodsham Street, Chester
Black and White Ornate
Design**

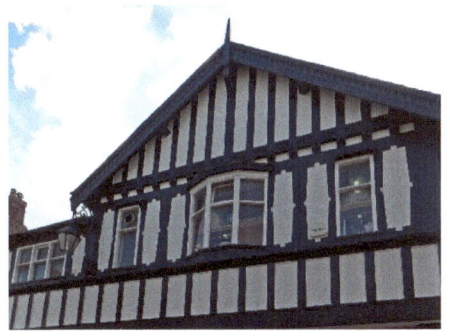

**Frodsham Street, Chester
Black and White Revival
Architecture**

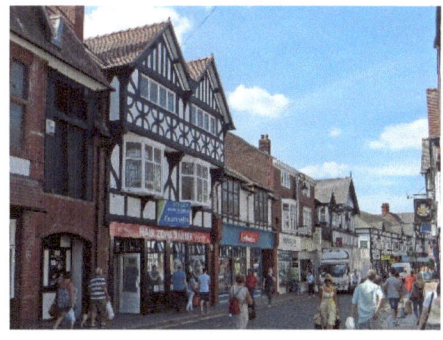

Frodsham Street, Chester

Chester A Photographic Glimpse

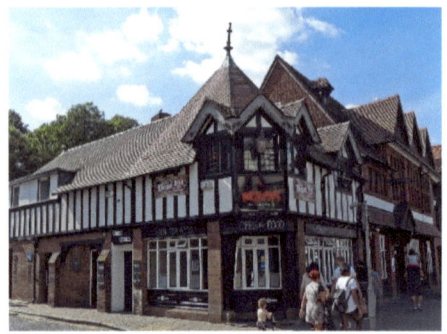

**Frodsham Street, Chester
Black and White Revival
Architecture**

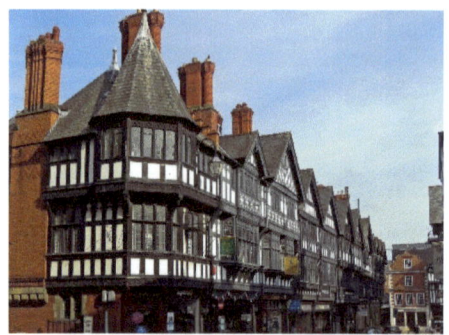

**Black & White Revival
Architecture St. Werburgh
Street, Chester**

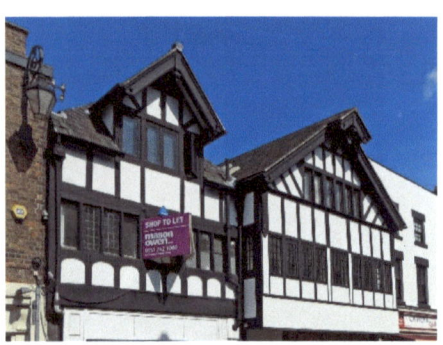

**Black & White Revival
Architecture St. Werburgh
Street, Chester**

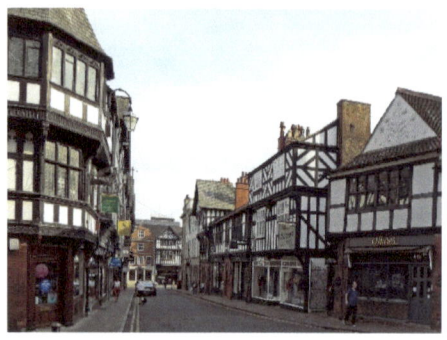

**Black & White Revival
Architecture St. Werburgh
Street, Chester**

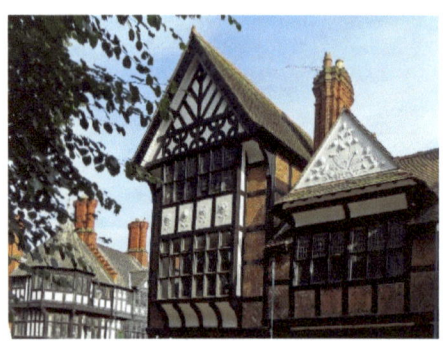

**Black & White Revival
Architecture St. Werburgh
Street, Chester**

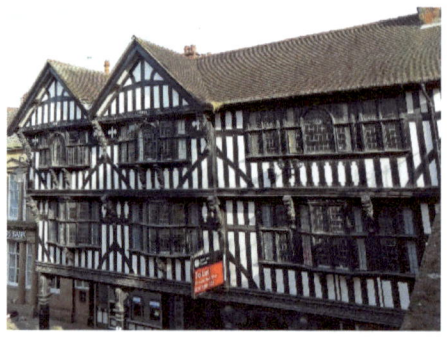

**Black & White Revival
Architecture**

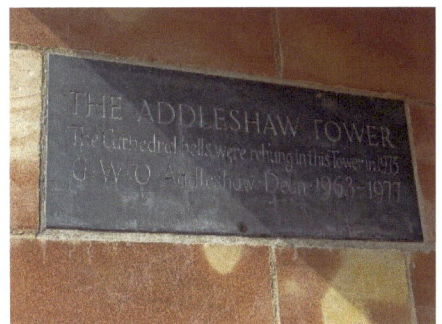

The Addleshaw Tower

"The Cathedral Bells were rehung in this Tower in 1975 G. W. O. Addleshaw Dean 1963 – 1977"

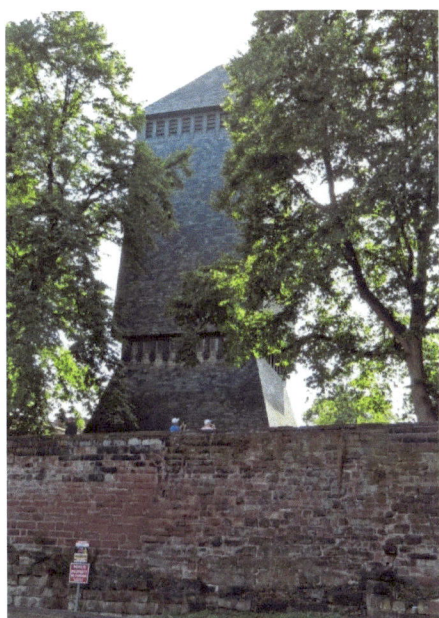

The Addleshaw Tower, Chester and City Walls

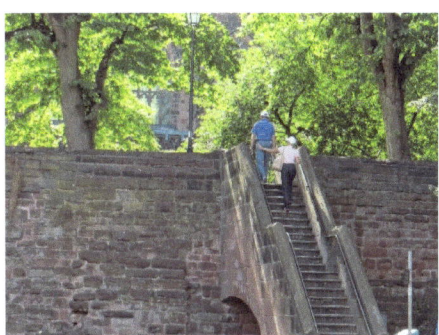

Steps to City Walls by Chester's Cathedral

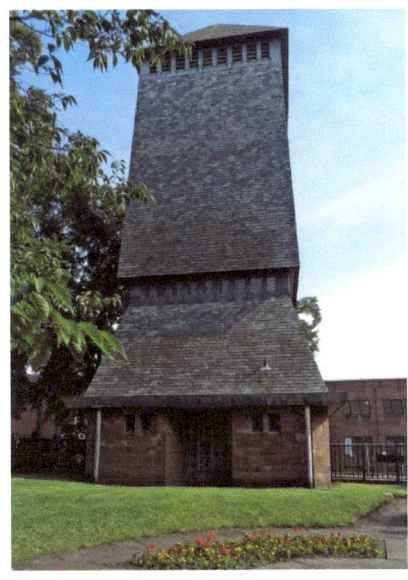

The Addleshaw Bell Tower, Chester - Front View

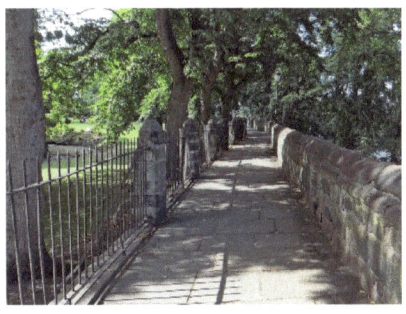

City Walls Walk by Chester's Cathedral

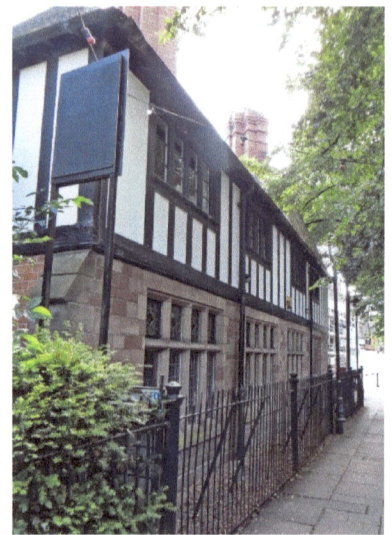

Bell Tower Walk, Chester

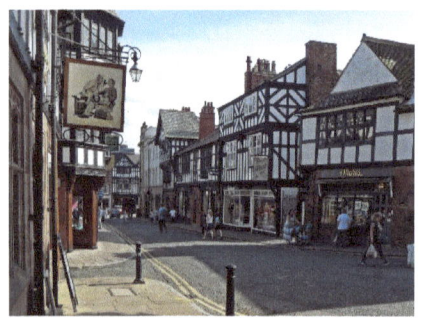

St. Werburgh Street, Chester Architecture

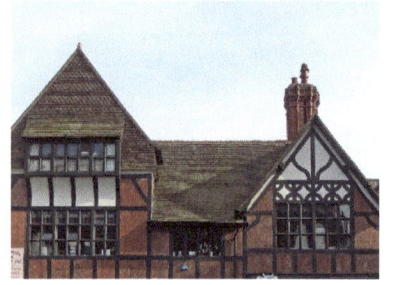

St. Werburgh Street, Chester Architecture

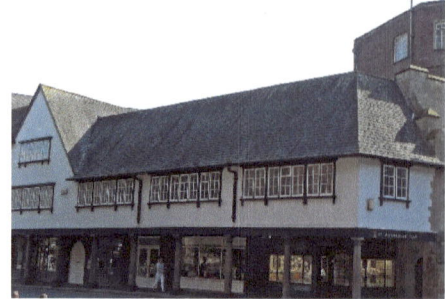

St. Werburgh Street, Chester

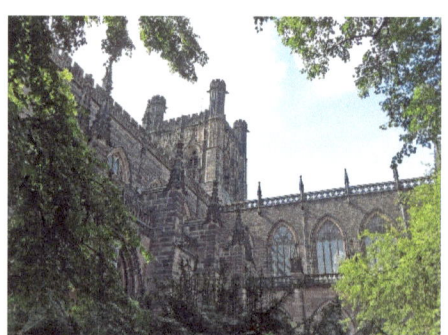

Chester Cathedral

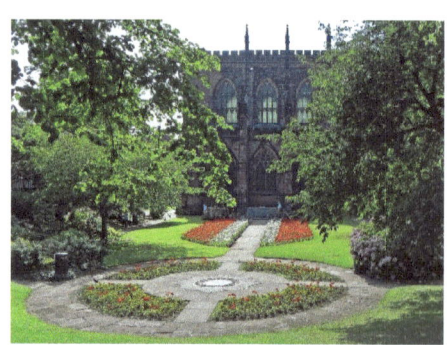

Chester Cathedral Remembrance Garden to Cheshire Regiment

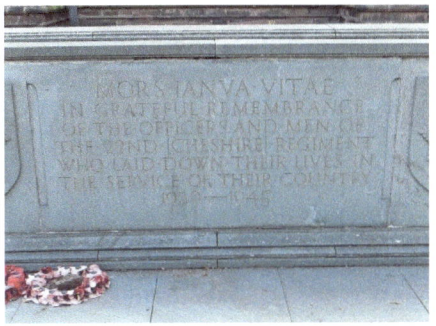

Chester Cathedral 22nd Cheshire Regiment Memorial

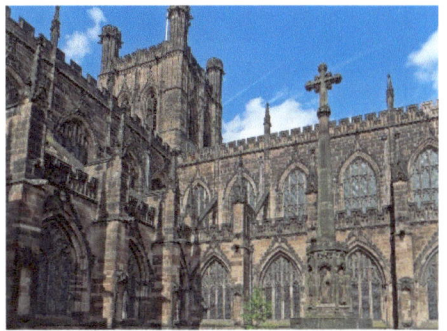

Chester Cathedral with Cross Memorial

"MORS – JANVA – VITAE

In grateful remembrance of the Officers and Men of the 22nd Cheshire Regiment who laid down their lives in the Service of their Country

1939 – 1945"

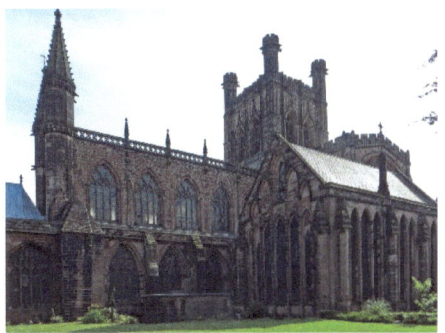

Chester Cathedral

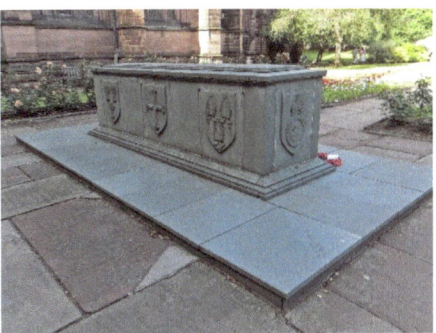

Chester Cathedral 22nd Cheshire Regiment Memorial

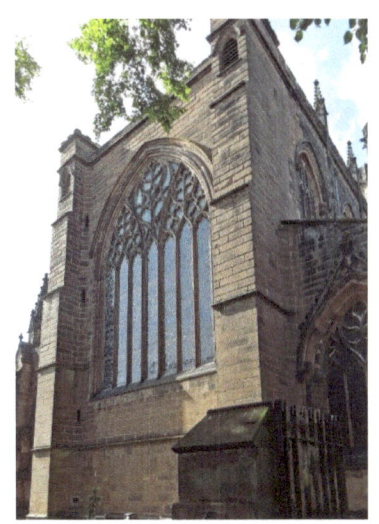

Chester Cathedral

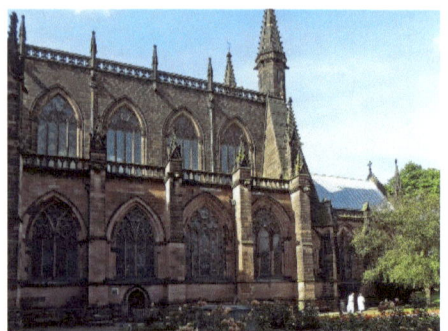
Chester Cathedral's view from the Garden of Remembrance

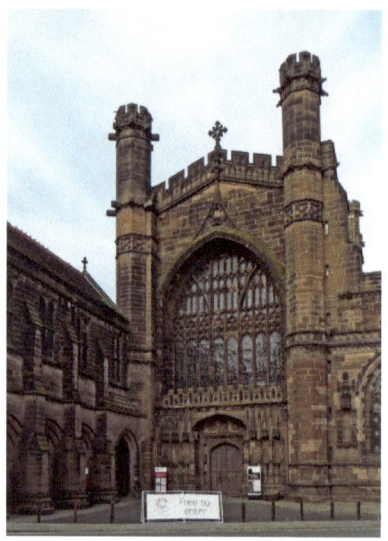
Chester Cathedral, Main Entrance

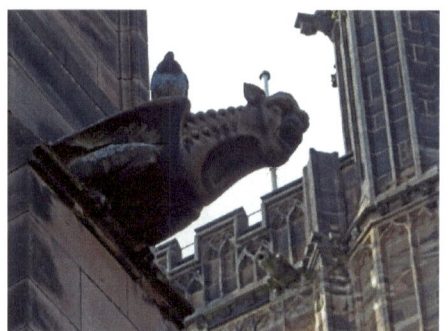
Winged Statue Chester Cathedral

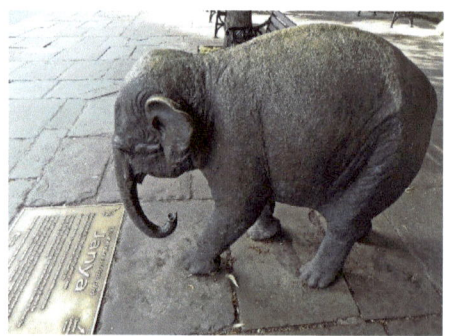
Janya

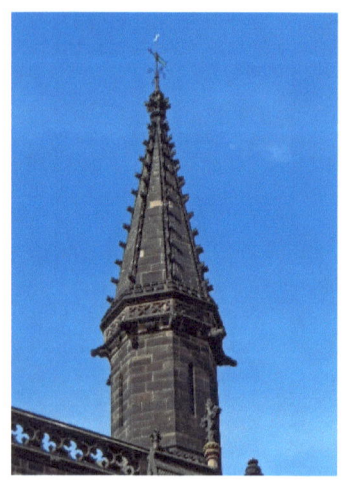
Turret, Chester Cathedral

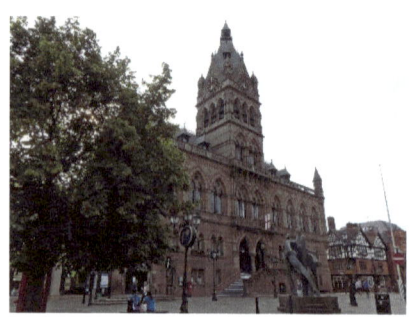
Chester Town Hall

Chester A Photographic Glimpse

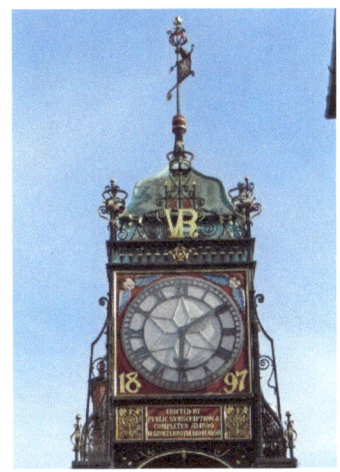

East Gate Clock, Chester

"Erected by public subscription and completed A.D. 1899 H. Stolteforth Mayor."

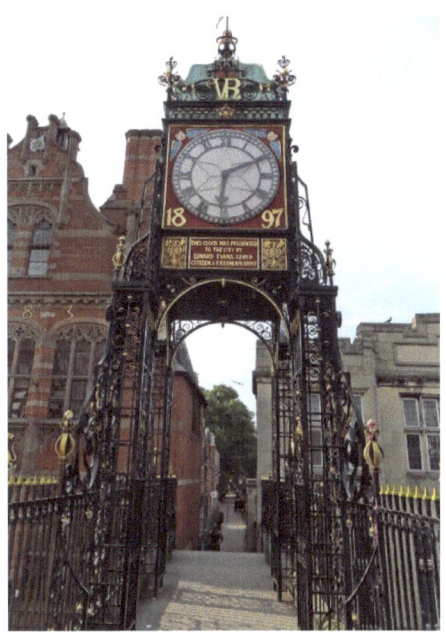

East Gate Clock, Chester.

"This clock was erected by Edward Evans-Lloyds Citizen and Freeman 1897"

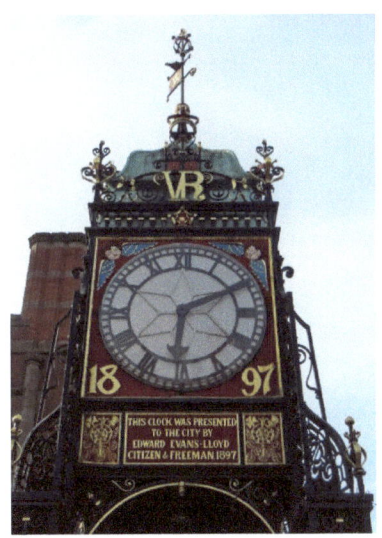

East Gate Clock

"This clock was erected by Edward Evans-Lloyds Citizen and Freeman 1897"

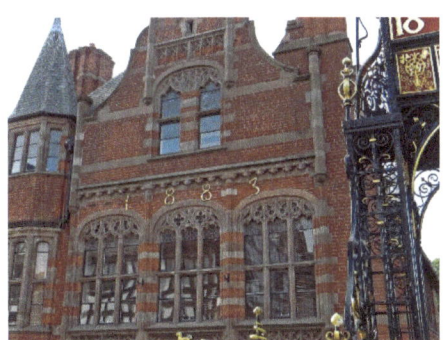

East Gate Street, Chester 1883 Architecture

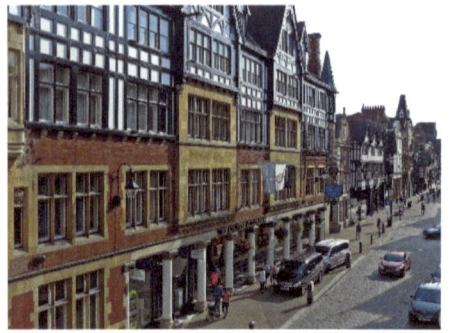
The Chester Grosvenor

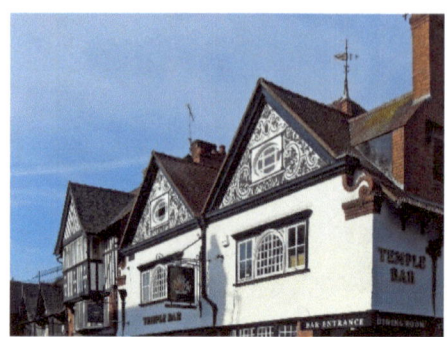
Temple Bar, Chester

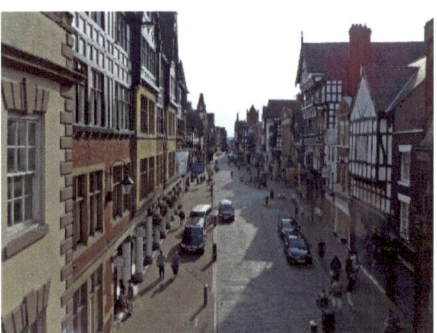
East Gate Street, Chester

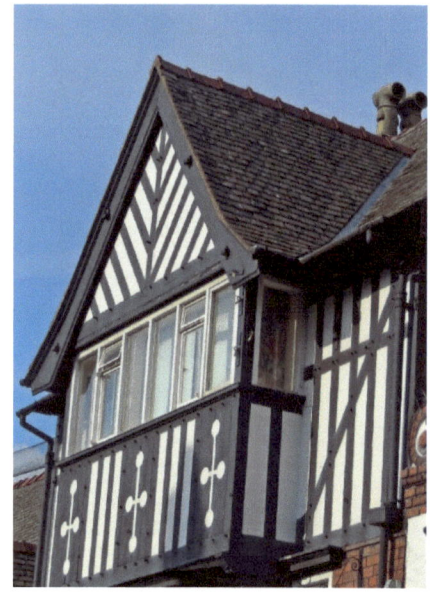
Frodsham Street Architecture

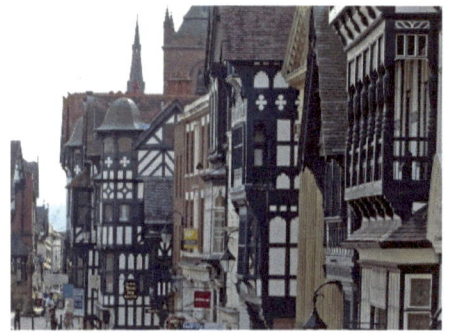
Architecture East Gate Street, Chester

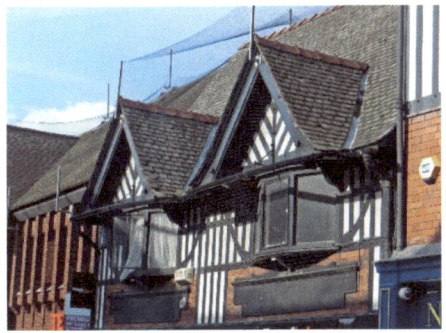
Frodsham Street Architecture

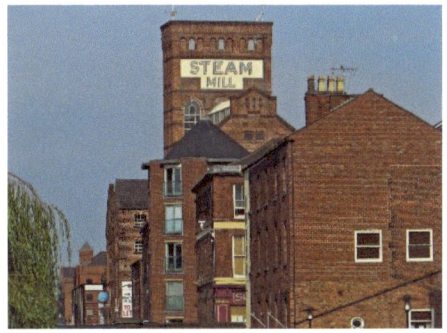
Steam Mill, Chester

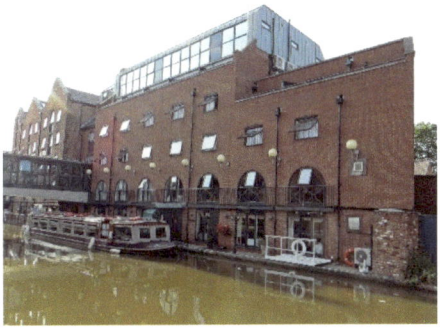
Mill Hotel and Spa, with Canal Barge, Chester

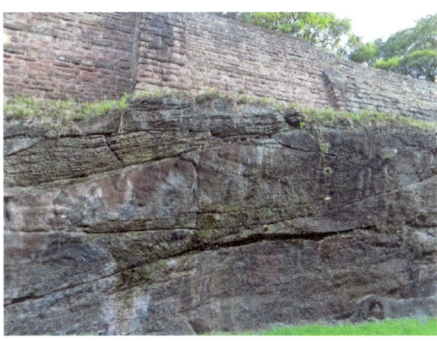
Chester City Walls from Canal

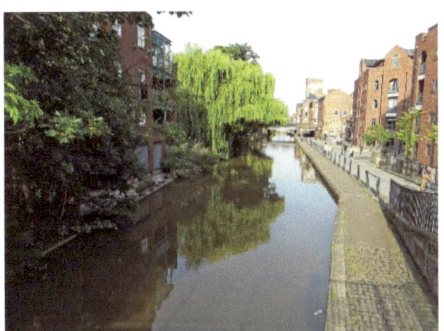
Shropshire Union Canal Main Line, Chester

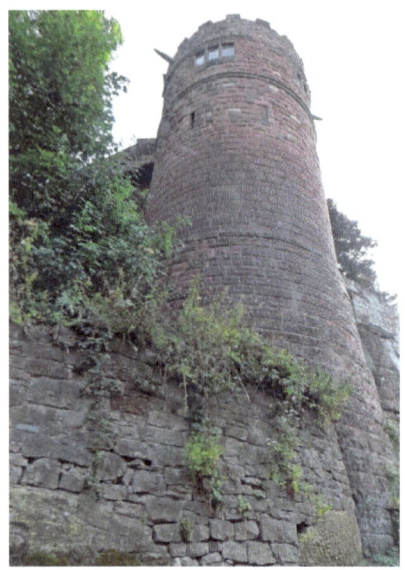

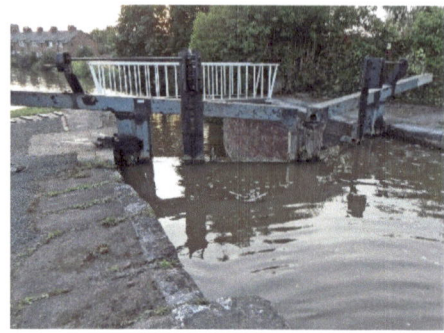

Chemistry Lock, Shropshire Union Canal, Chester

North-East Tower Chester Walls, King Charles I Tower, Phoenix Tower, Newton Tower

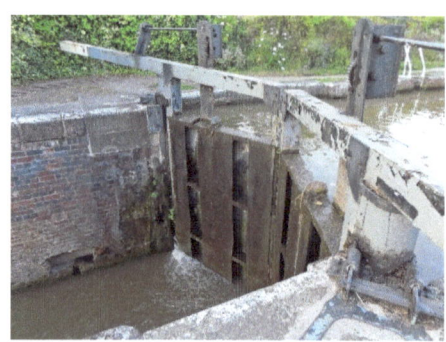

Chemistry Lock, Shropshire Union Canal, Chester

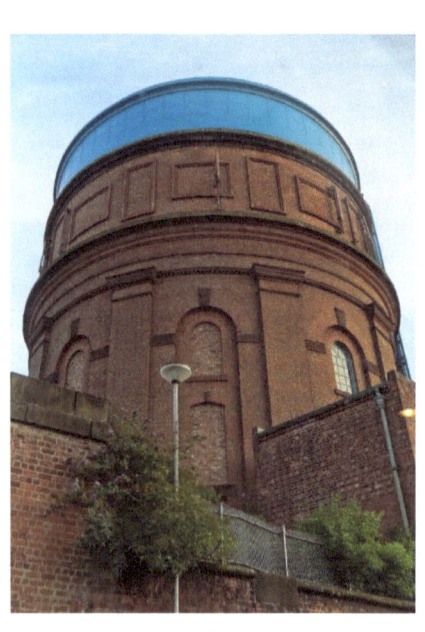

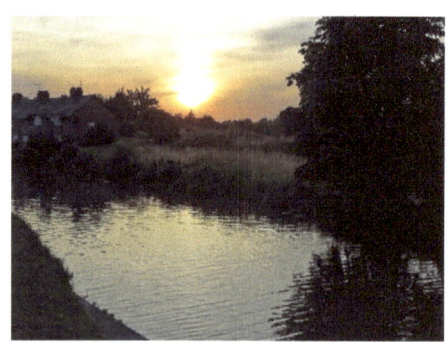

Sunset at Chemistry Lock, Cheshire

Broughton Water Tower, Chester

Chester A Photographic Glimpse

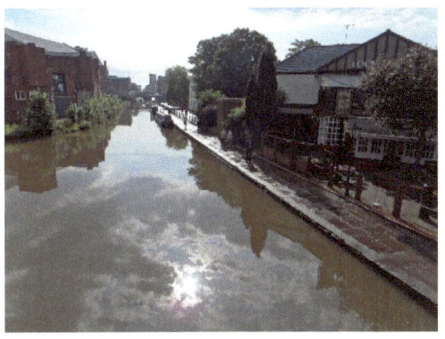

After the rain, Chester Canal

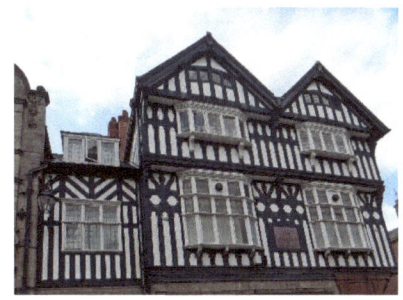

Black and White Revival Architecture Chester

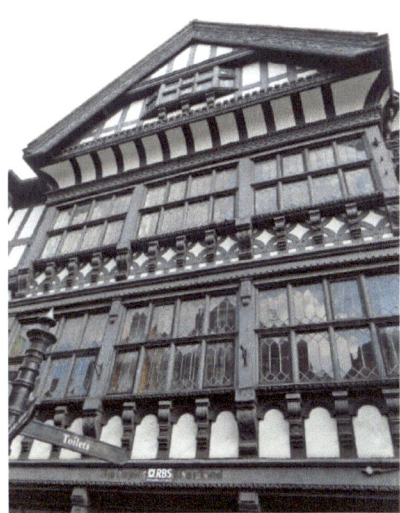

Black and White Revival Architecture Chester

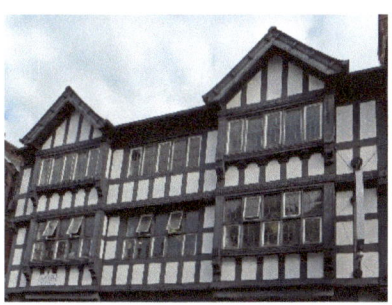

Black and White Revival Architecture Chester

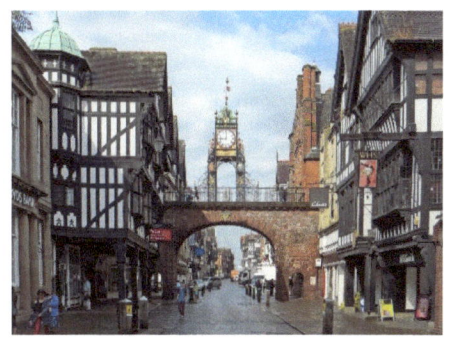

East Gate Street and East Gate Clock

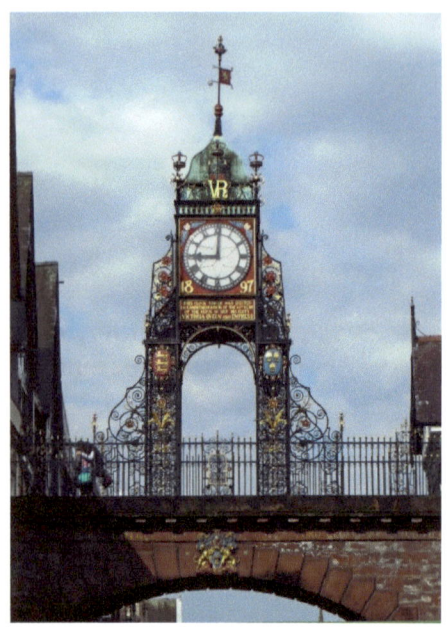

East Gate Clock

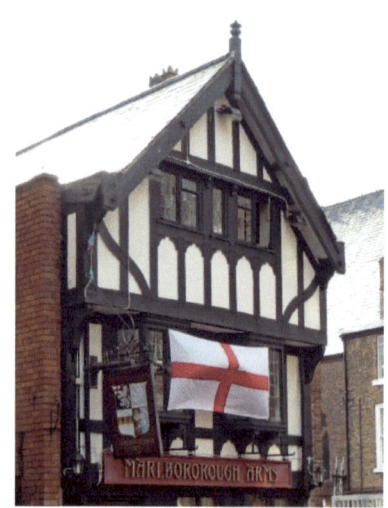

Marlborough Arms, East Gate Street, Chester

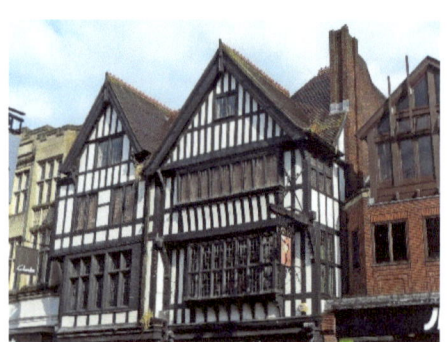

Black and White Revival Architecture

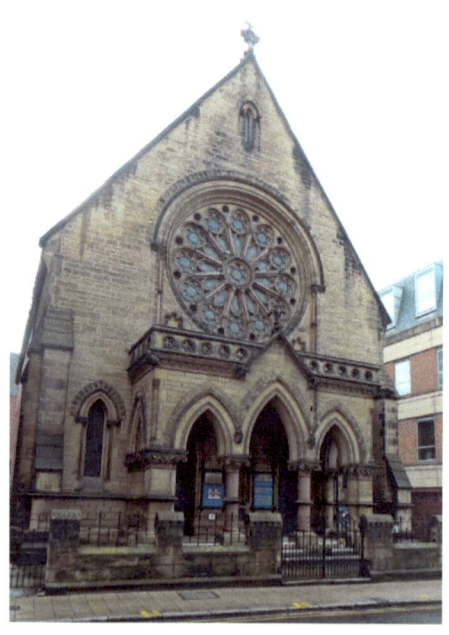

Welsh Presbyterian Church, City Road, Chester

Chester A Photographic Glimpse

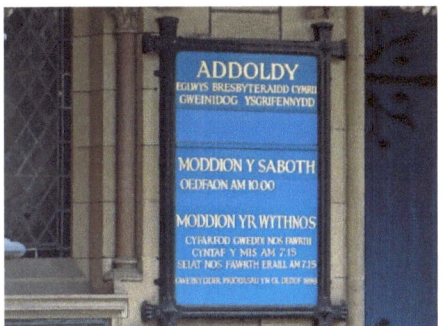

Welsh Presbyterian Church, City Road, Chester

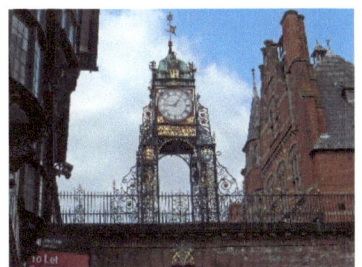

East Gate Street Clock, Chester

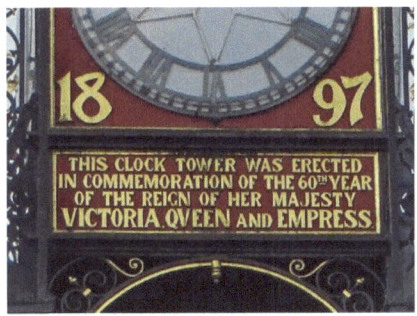

East Gate Street Clock, Chester

"This Tower was erected in commemoration of the 60th Year of the Reign of Her Majesty Victoria, Queen and Empress."

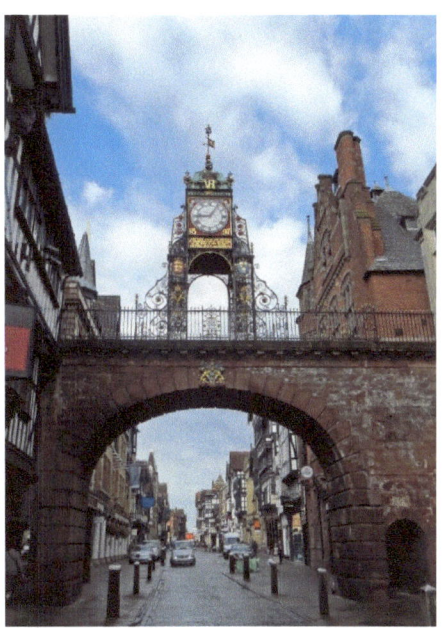

Arch East Gate Street with Clock above

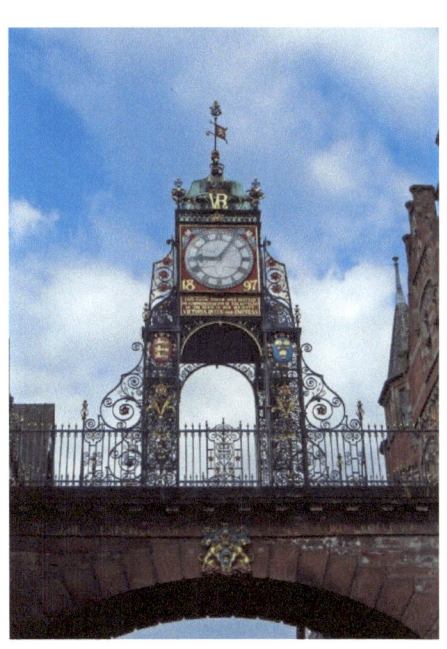

East Gate Clock Ironwork

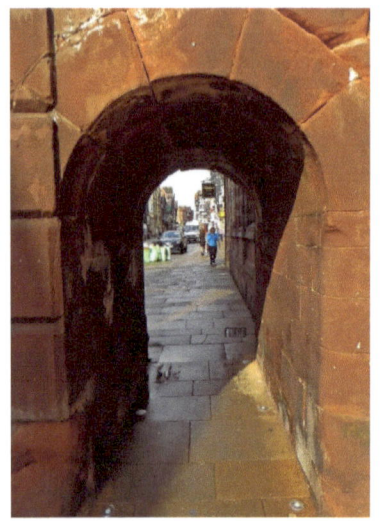

East Gate Small Archway

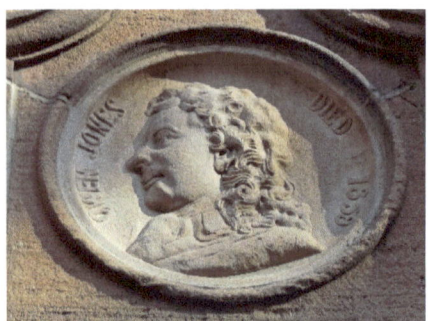

Owen Jones Died 1858 Stone Plaque

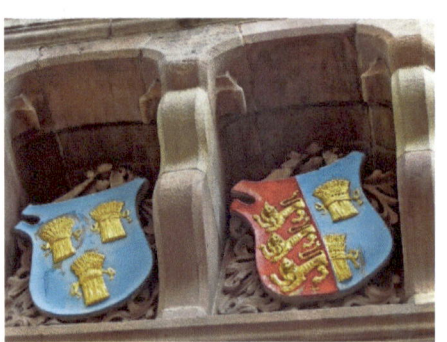

Colourful Shields Chester

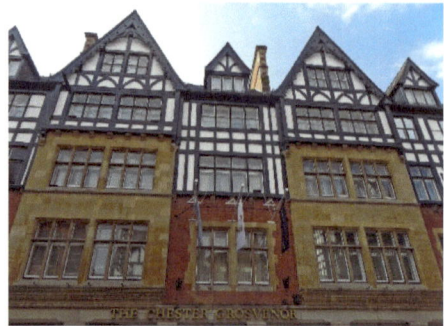

The Chester Grosvenor, Hotel

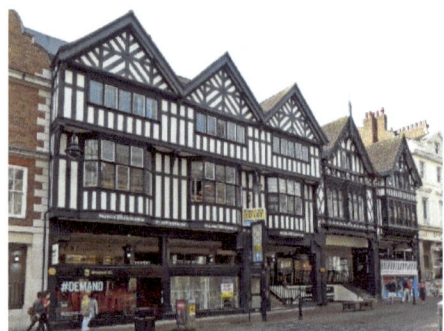

East Gate Street, Black and White Buildings

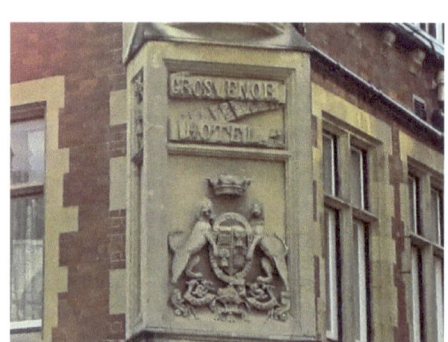

Grosvenor Hotel Emblem, Chester

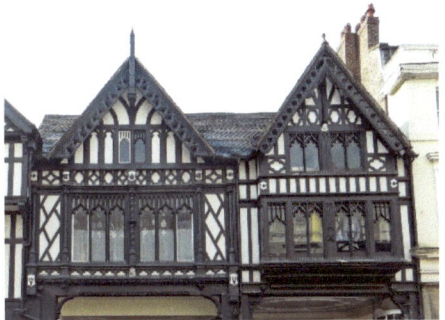

East Gate Street Black and White Buildings

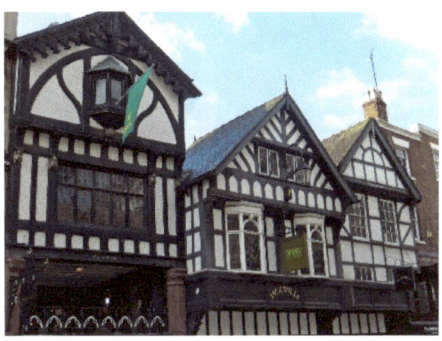

East Gate Street Black and White Revival Architecture

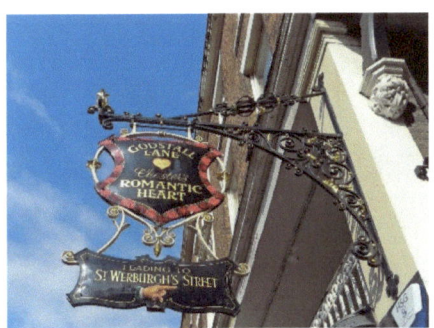

Godstall Lane Sign

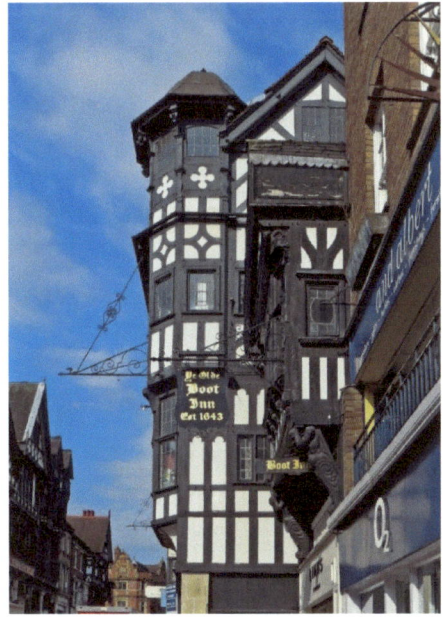

East Gate Street Black and White Revival Architecture

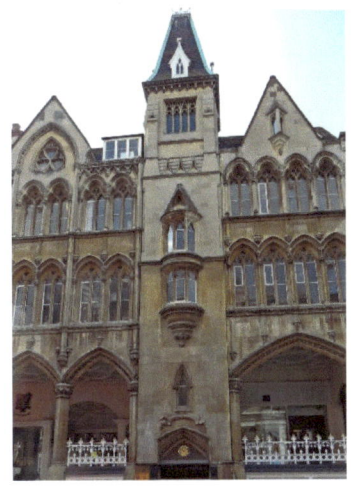

East Gate Street Architectural Building

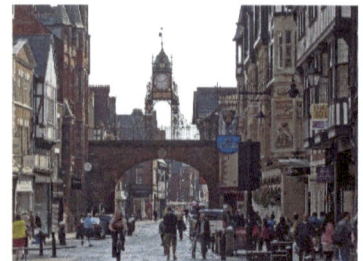
East Gate and Clock, Street Level

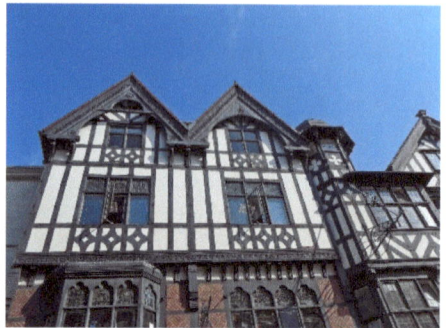
Black and White Revival Architecture

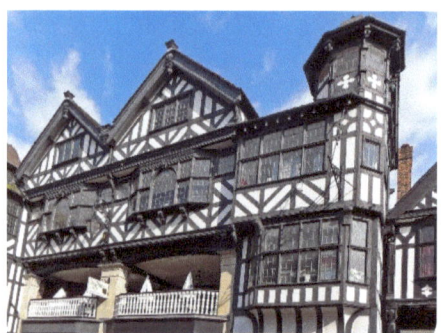
East Gate Black and White Revival Buildings

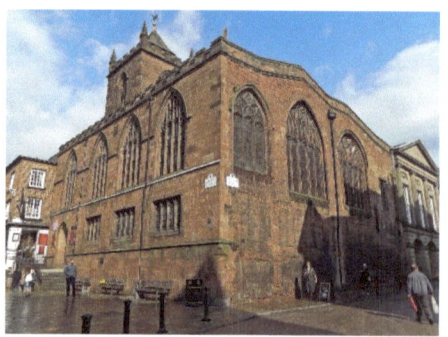
The Guild Church of St. Peter at the Cross, Chester

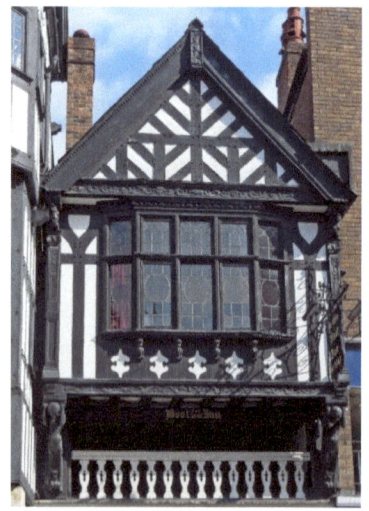
Boot Inn, Established 1643, Chester

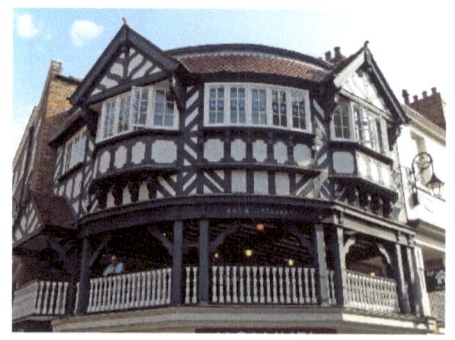
Corner of East Gate Street and Bridge Street, Revival Architecture

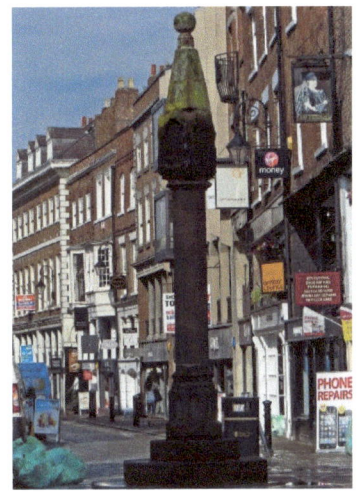
Chester Cross

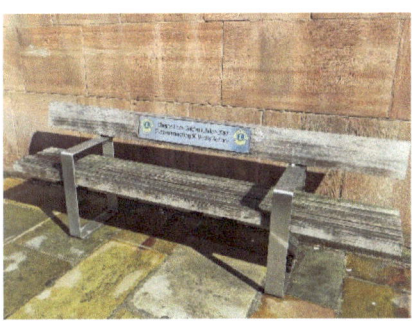
Chester Lions Jubilee Bench adjacent to the Chester Cross

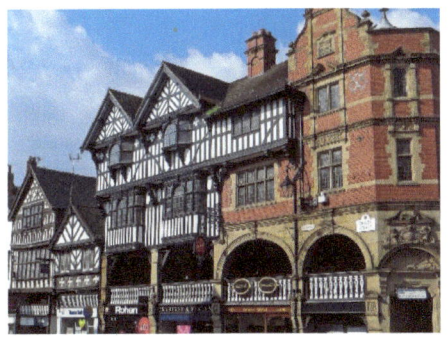
Bridge Street with Black and White Buildings

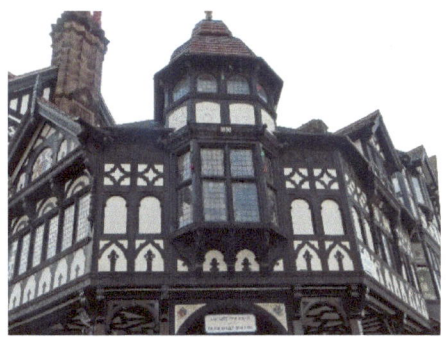
Black and White Revival Buildings 1888

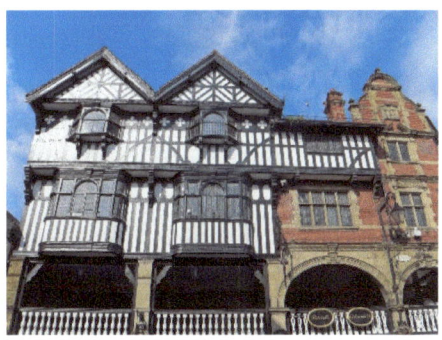
Black and White Revival Buildings, Bridge Street, Chester

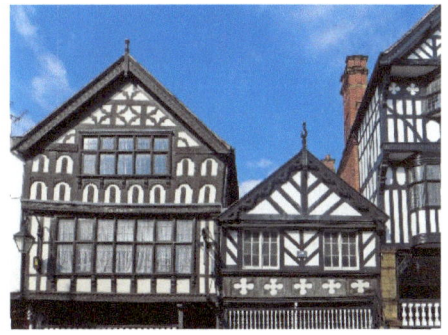
TC 1664 Black and White Buildings, Bridge Street, Chester

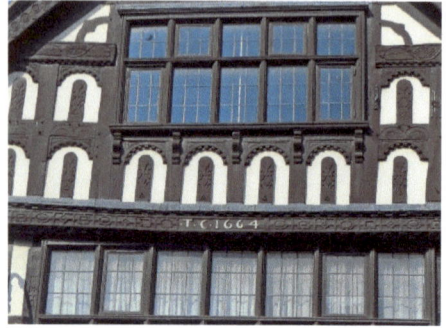

TC 1664 Black and White Buildings Detail, Bridge Street, Chester

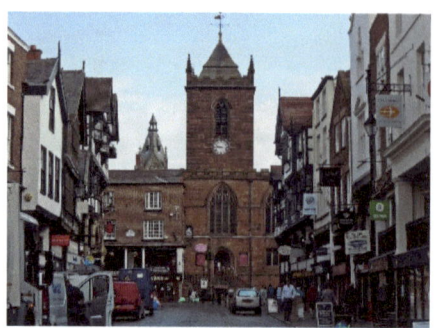

Bridge Street, looking towards the Guild of St. Peter at the Cross Church

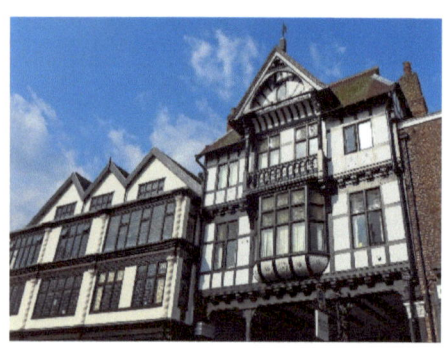

Bridge Street, Black and White Buildings

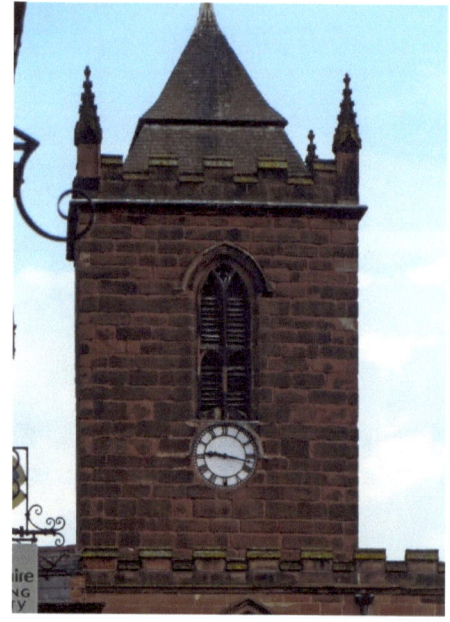

St. Peter at the Cross Church, Chester, Clock Tower

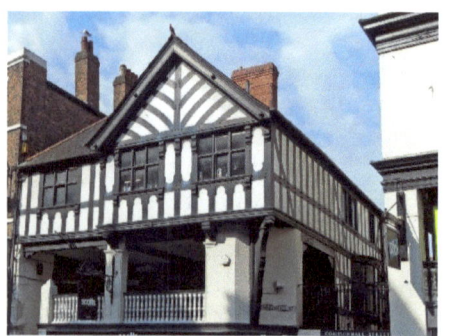

Bridge Street, Black and White Buildings

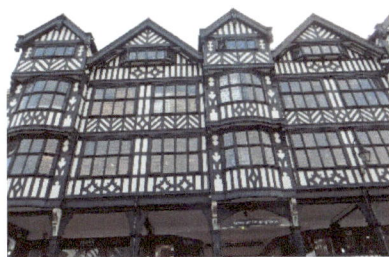

Grosvenor Shopping Centre, Chester

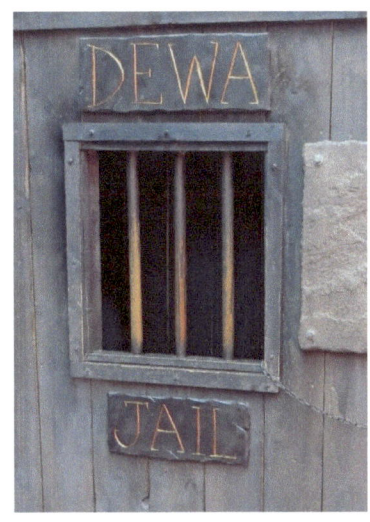

Dewa Roman Experience Jail

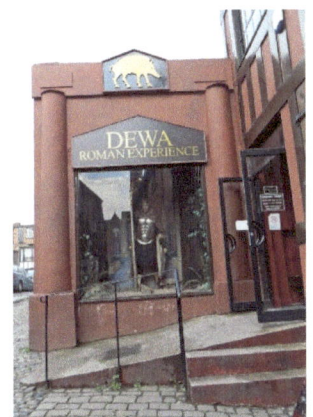

Dewa Roman Experience

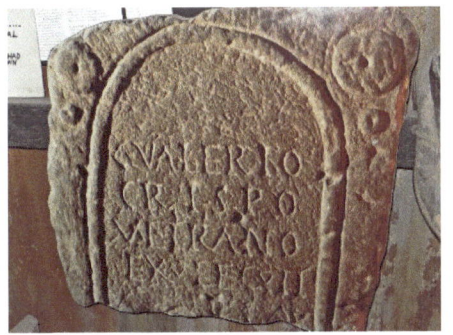

Dewa Roman Experience Roman Tablet

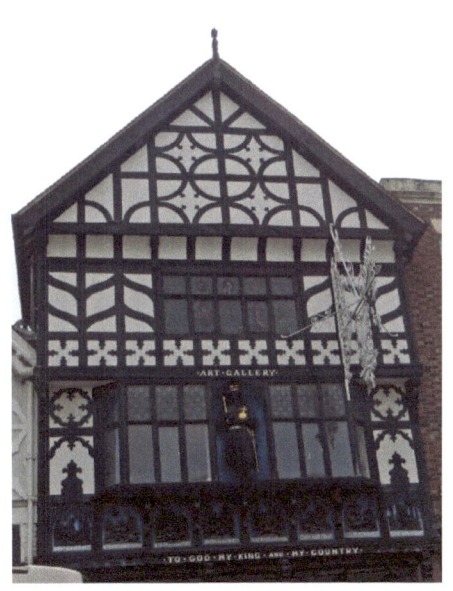

Bridge Street Art Gallery, Chester

Chester A Photographic Glimpse

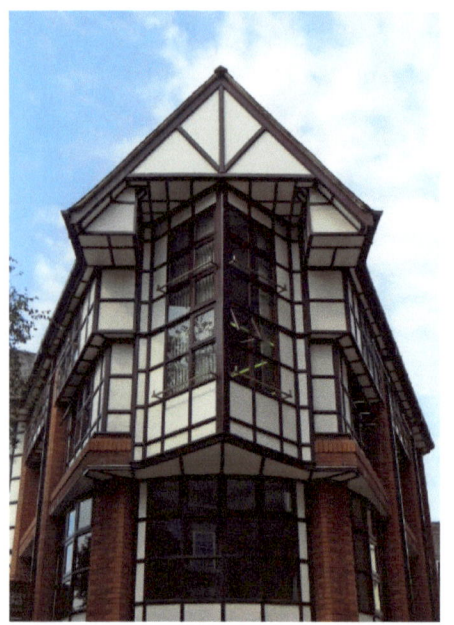

Bridge Street, Modern Black and White Architecture

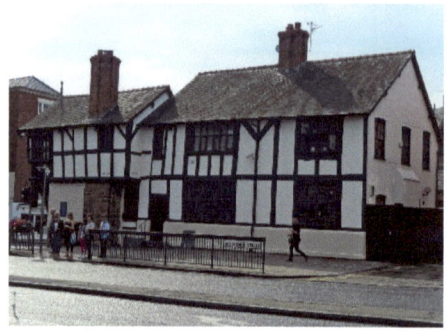

Grosvenor Street, Chester

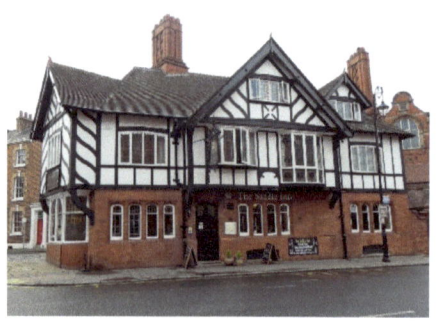

The Saddle Inn, Chester

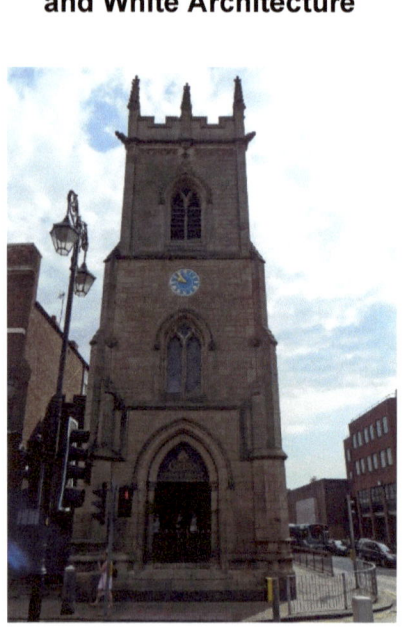

St. Michael's Church, Chester, History & Heritage Centre

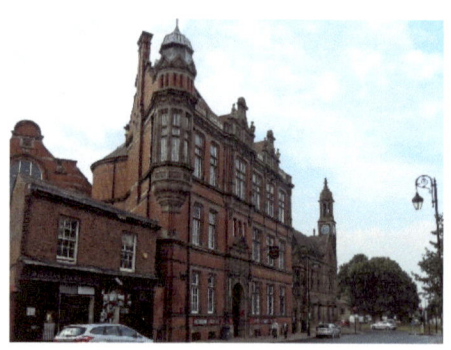

Grosvenor Museum Chester 1886

Chester A Photographic Glimpse

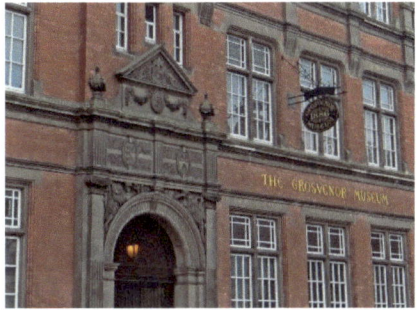

Grosvenor Museum, Exterior Architecture

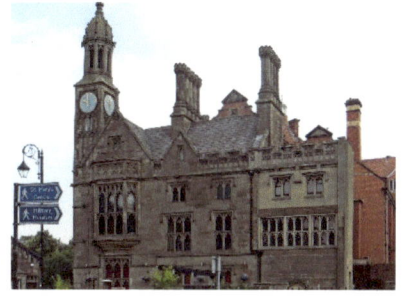

Grosvenor Museum, Chester

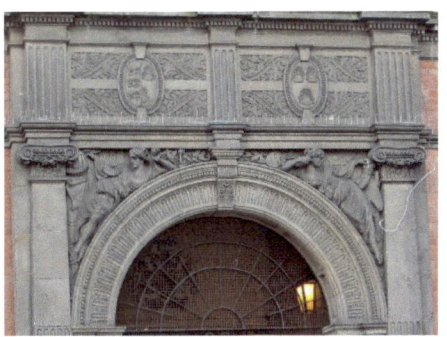

Grosvenor Museum Exterior Architecture, Chester

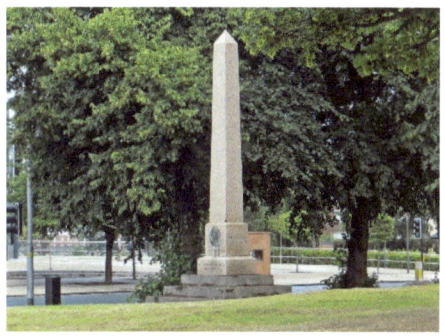

Matthew Henry Obelisk

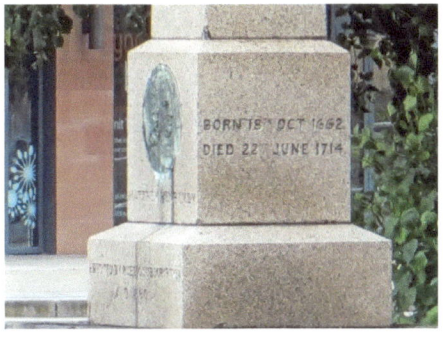

Cenotaph to Matthew Henry, Chester

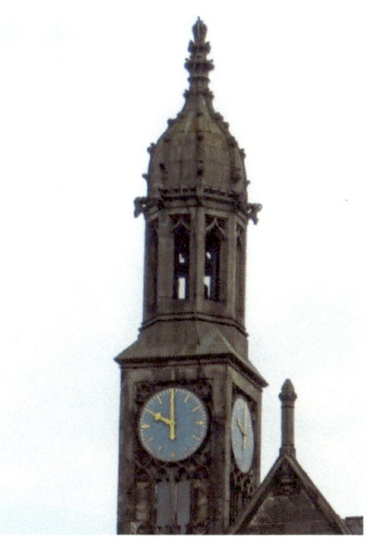

Grosvenor Museum Clock, Chester

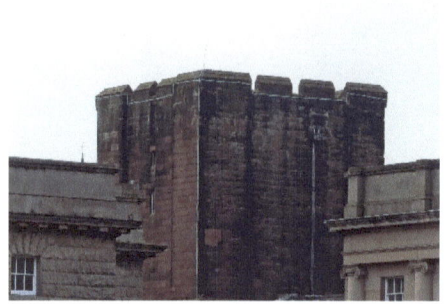

Tower, Chester Castle

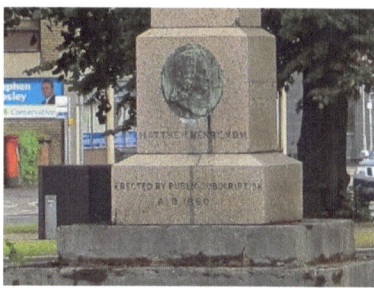

Mathew Henry Obelisk, on roundabout near Grosvenor Museum, Chester

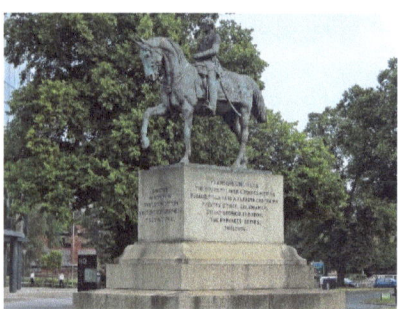

Field Marshal Stapleton Cotton, 1st Viscount Combermere GCB, GCH, KSI, PC Equestrian Statue

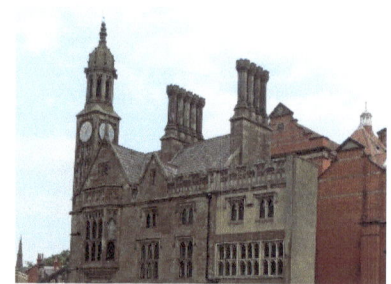

Clock Tower and Chimneys of the Grosvenor Museum, Chester

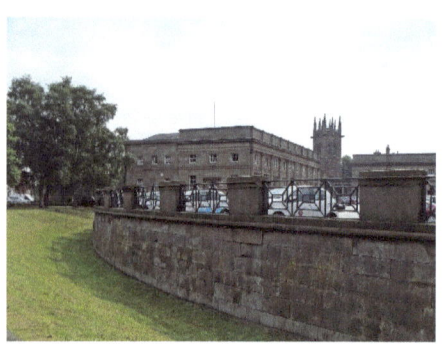

Chester's Military Museum

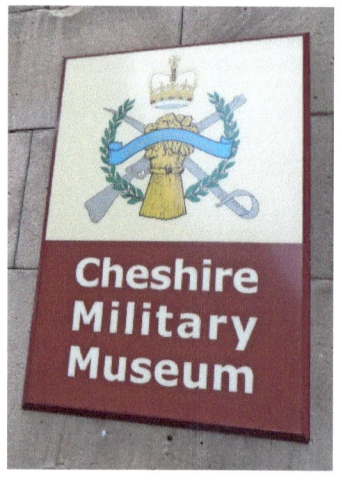

Cheshire Military Museum

Chester A Photographic Glimpse

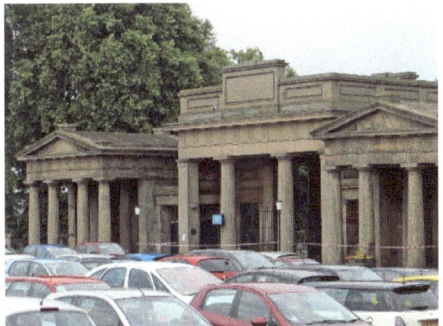

The Propylaeum, Chester Castle

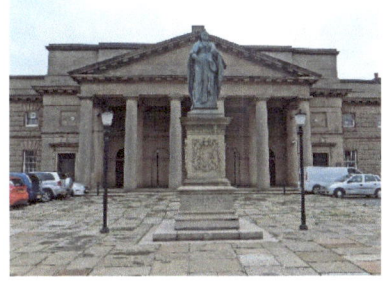

Queen Victoria Statue Chester Castle

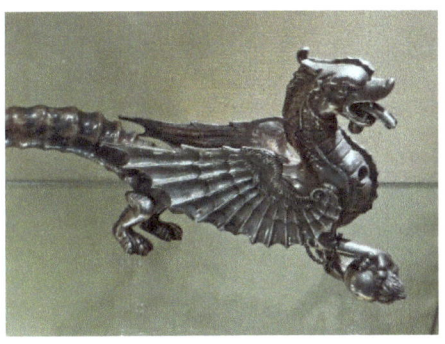

Winged Dragon, Cheshire Military Museum

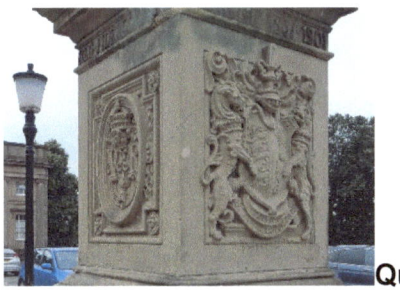

Queen Victoria's Statue Embellishments and Crests, Chester's Castle

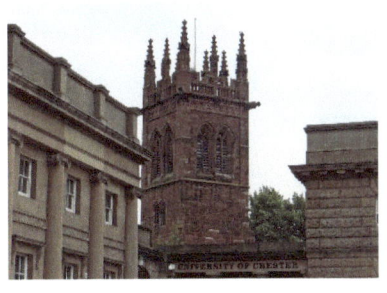

St. Mary's Church, Tower, Chester behind the University of Chester's entrance

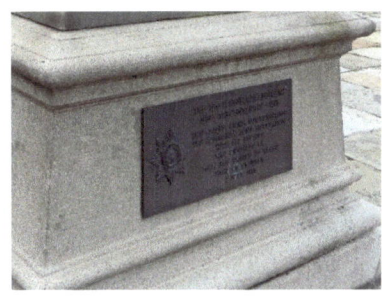

The 22nd Cheshire Regiment, Plaque, Queen Victoria's Statue Chester Castle

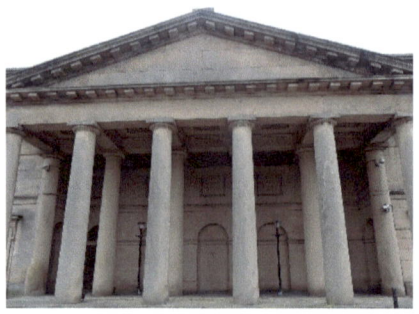

Chester's Crown Court situated next to Chester's Castle.

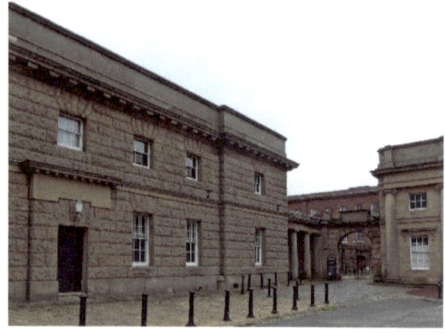

Chester Castle Entrance

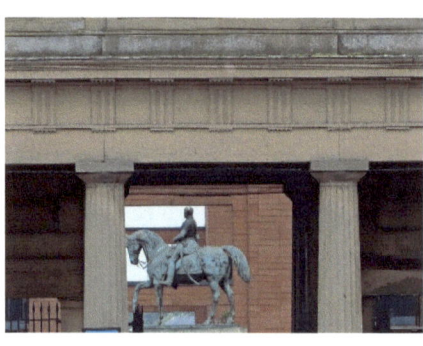

Statue of Field Marshall Stapleton Cotton through the Propylaeum, from the Statue of Queen Victoria

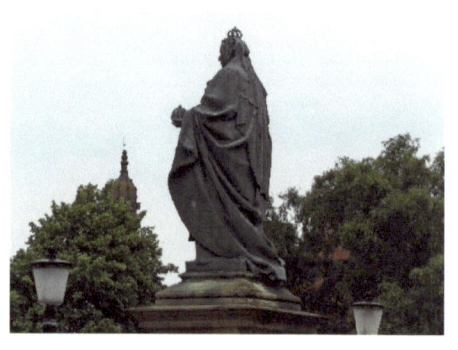

Queen Victoria's Statue from the rear

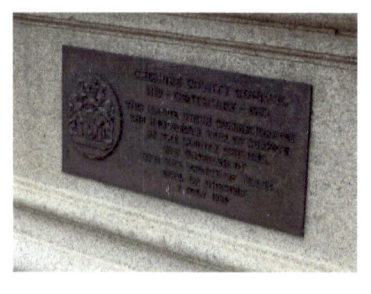

Cheshire County Council Hundredth Centenary Plaque

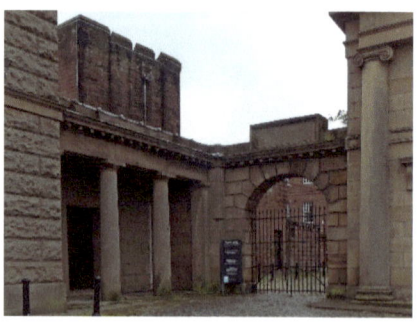

Archway to Chester's Castle

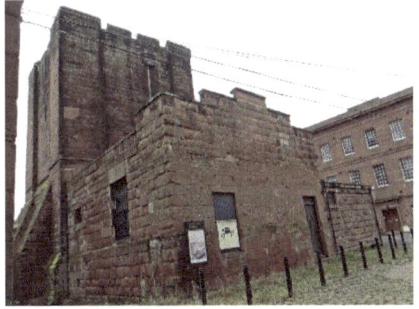

Chester's Tower and Castle

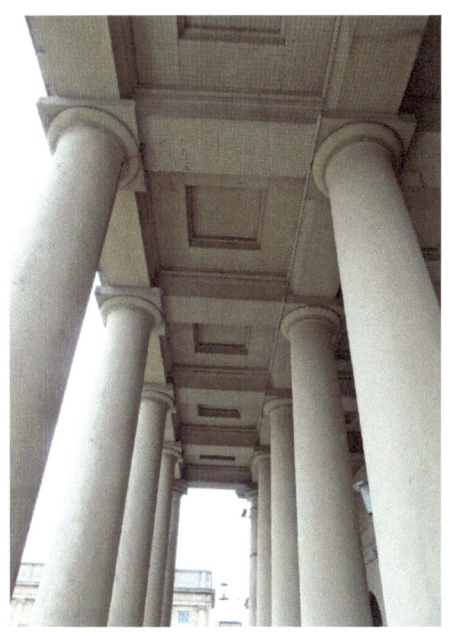

Portico, Chester Castle and Crown Courts

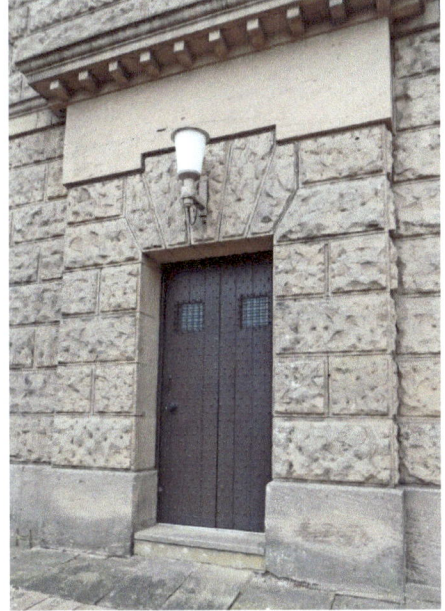

Fortified Prison Door, Chester Castle

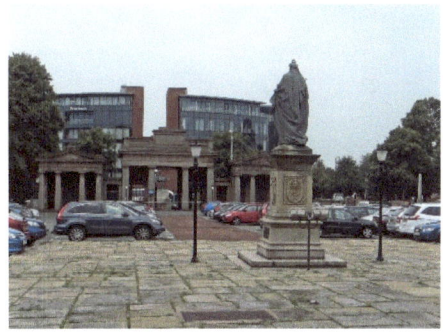

Forecourt, Chester's Castle and Crown Court with Queen Victoria's Statue

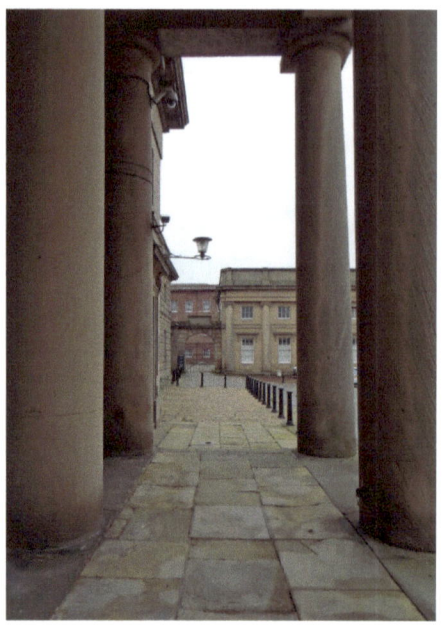

Portico Chester's Castle

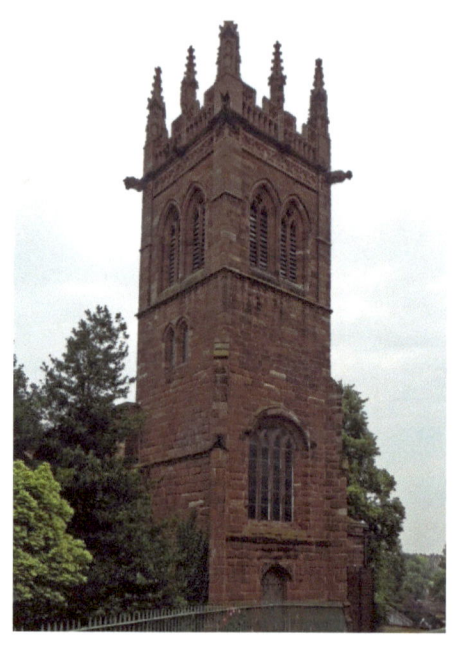

St. Mary's Church Tower, Chester

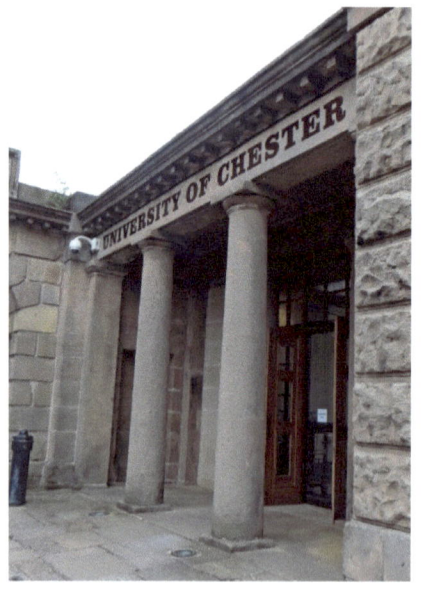

University of Chester Entrance

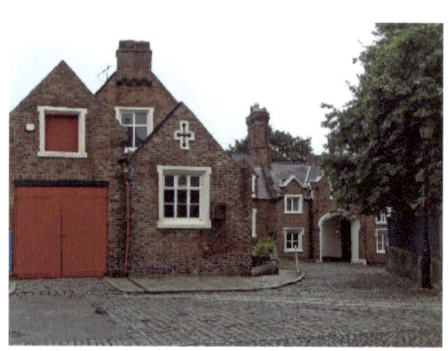

Architecture opposite St. Mary's Church, Chester

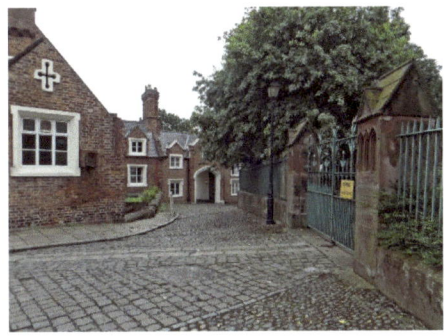

St Mary's Church Gates, Chester

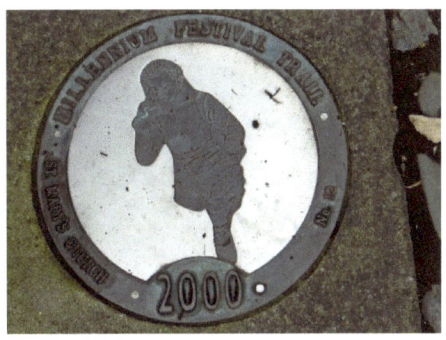

St. Mary's Church Millennium Festive Trail Plaque 2000

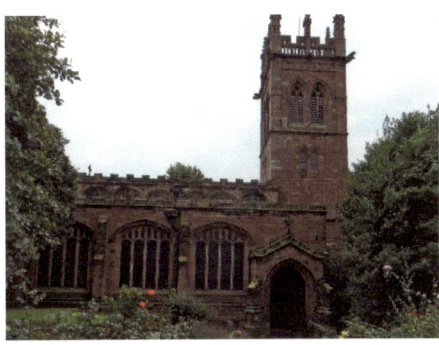

St. Mary's Church Front, Chester

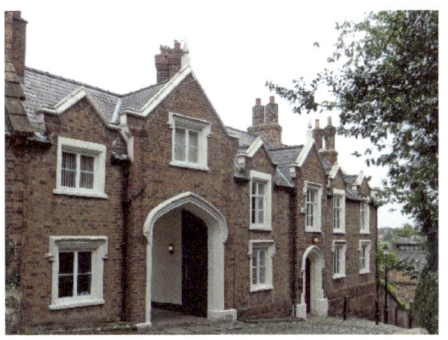

Architecture, Chester

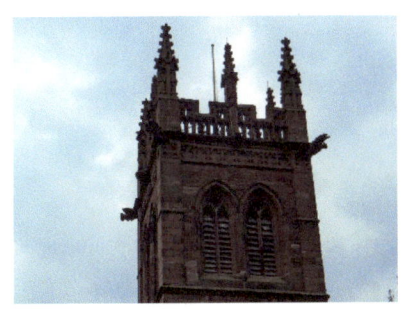

St. Mary's Church, Tower Details

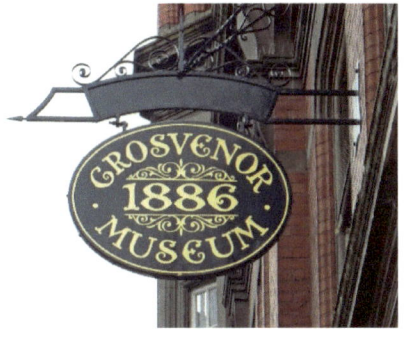

Grosvenor 1886 Museum Plaque

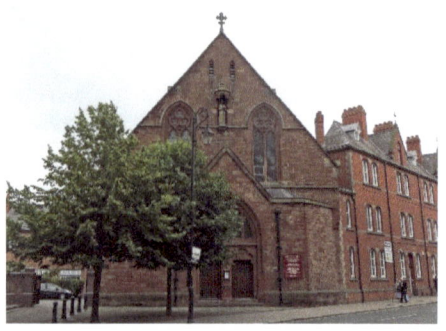

Catholic Church, St. Francis of Assisi

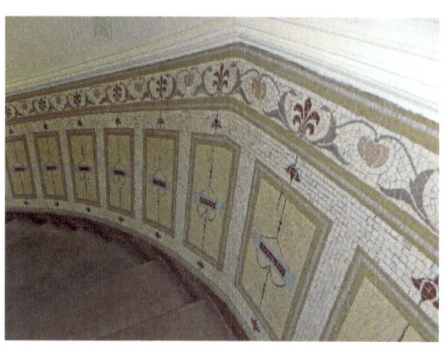

Grosvenor Museum, Mosaic on Staircase

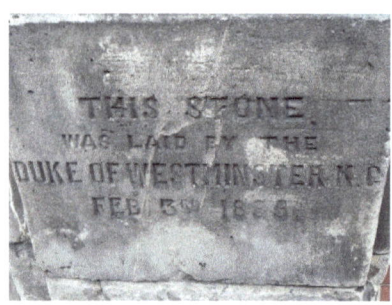

Foundation Stone, Grosvenor Museum

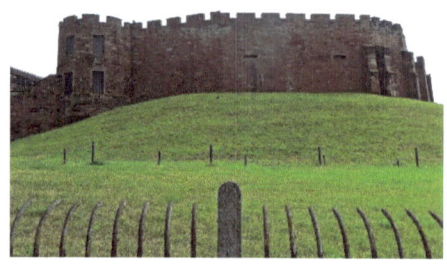

Chester Castle Walls

"This stone was laid by the Duke of Westminster K.G. Feb 3rd 1885",

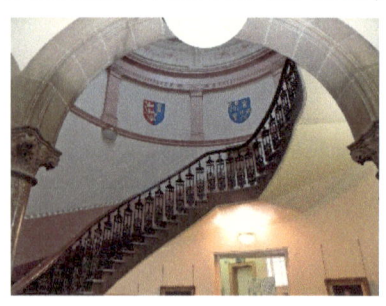

Grosvenor Museum, Entrance Staircase

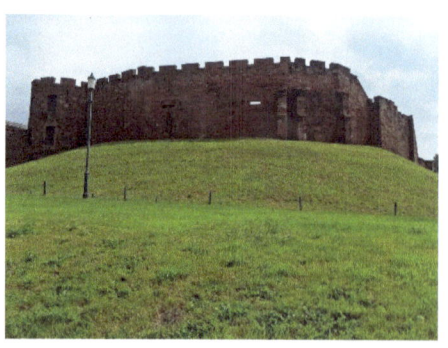

Chester Castle Exterior Profile

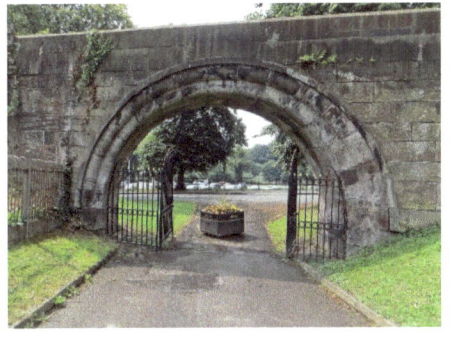

Castle Drive Bridge, Chester Castle

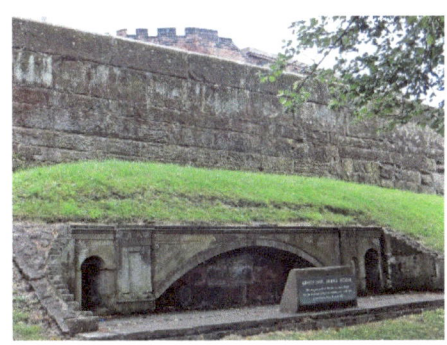

Grosvenor Bridge Model, Chester

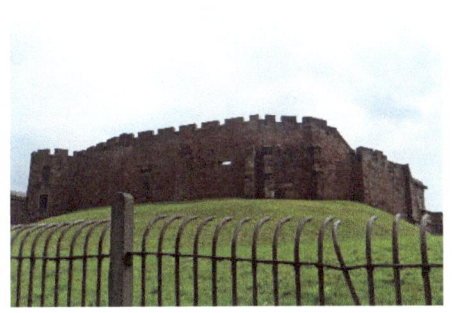

Chester's Castle Fortifications and Walls

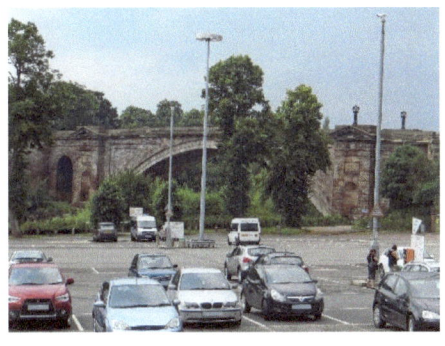

Grosvenor Bridge, Chester

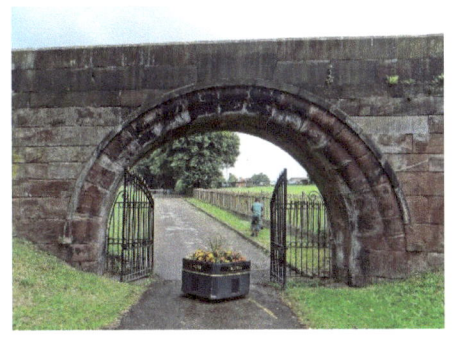

Castle Drive Bridge

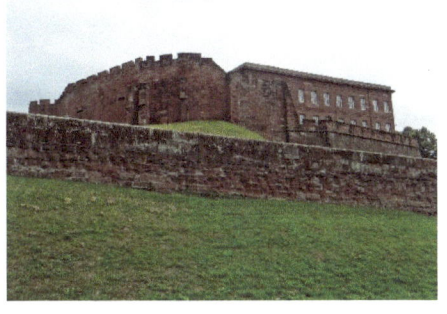

City Wall and Chester Castle

Chester A Photographic Glimpse

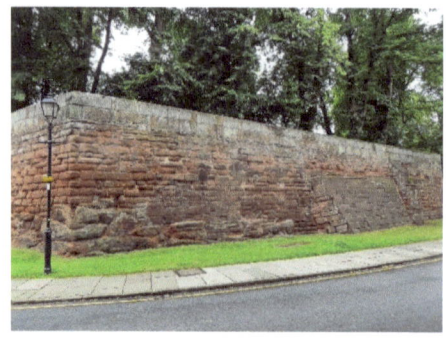

City Walls, Chester

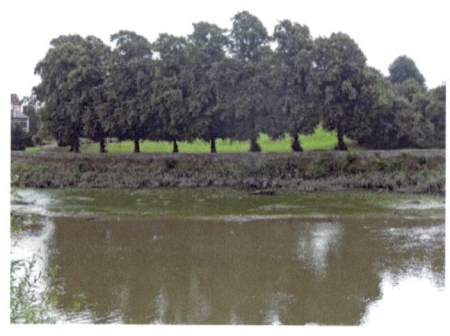

Trees along the River Dee

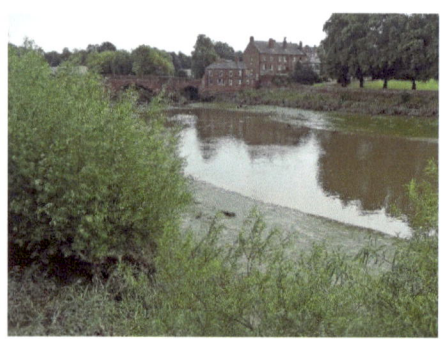

River Dee, by Handbridge

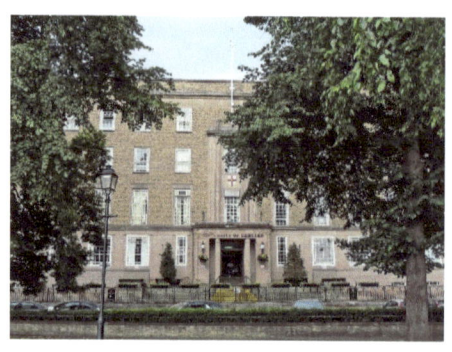

University of Chester

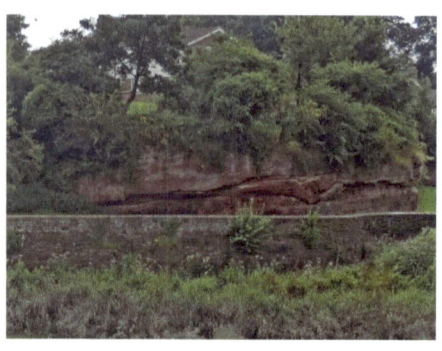

Rock Formation by River Dee

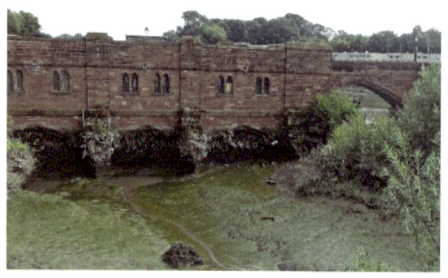

Handbridge, Chester

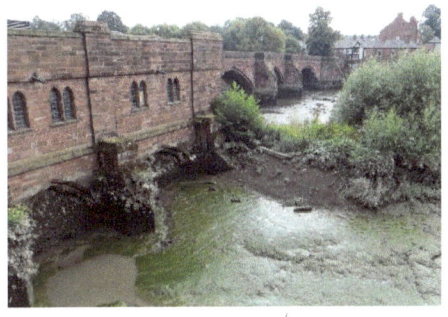

Handbridge, Chester and River Dee

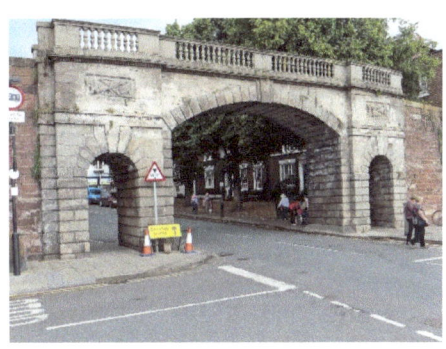

The Bridgegate, Chester

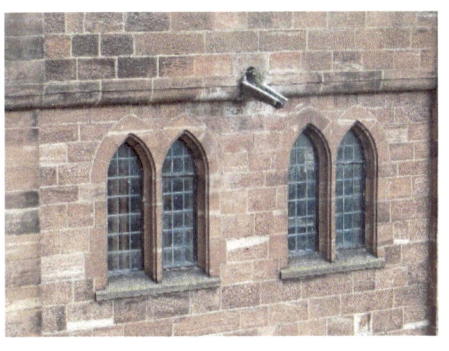

Handbridge, Chester Windows Architecture

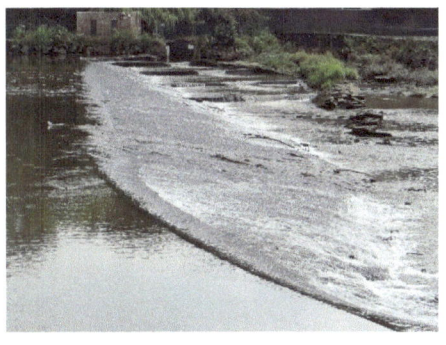

Chester Weir

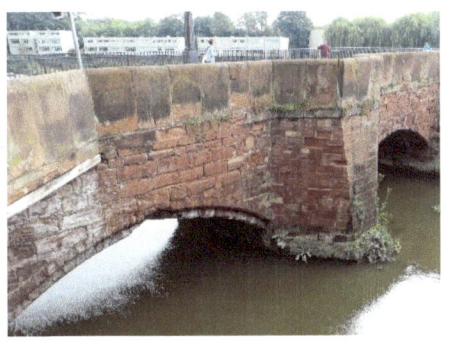

Handbridge Chester, Arches

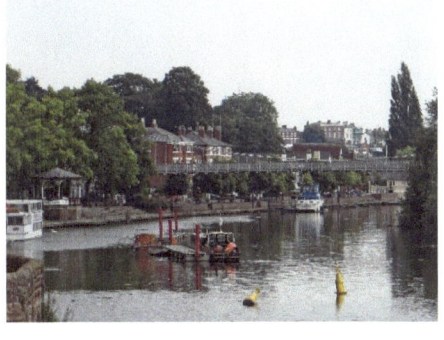

View of the Groves, from Handbridge

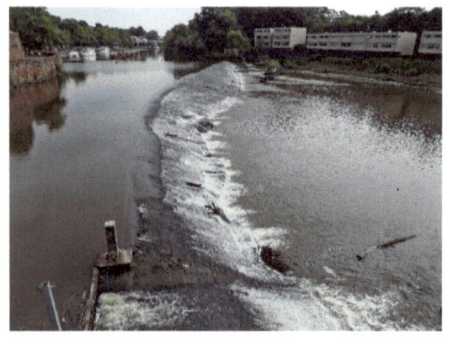

River Dee at Chester Weir

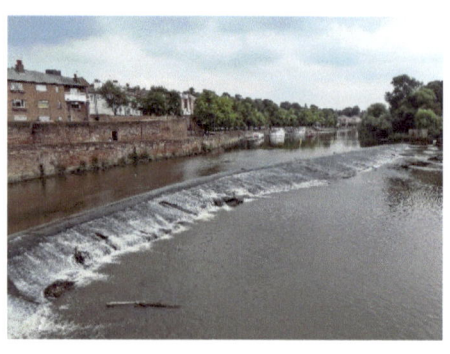

City Walls along River Dee

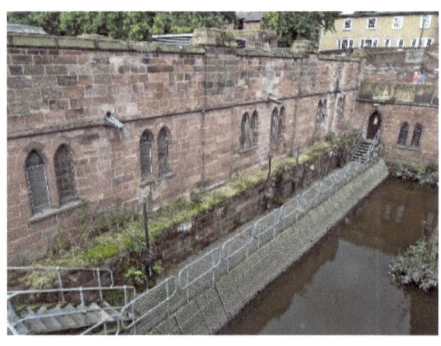

Handbridge Building

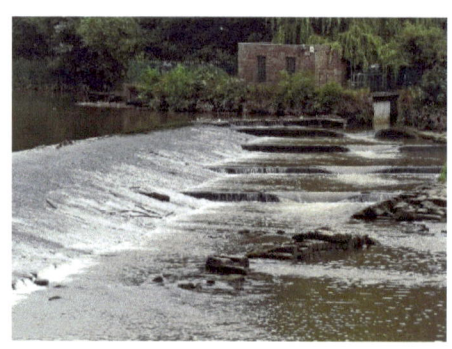

River Dee, Chester Weir

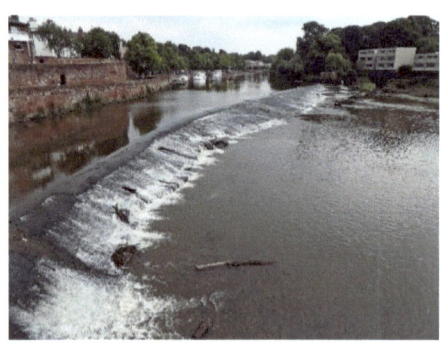

Chester Weir and River Dee

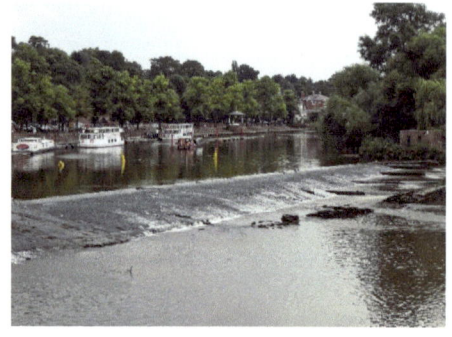

River Boats, Chester's River Dee

Chester A Photographic Glimpse

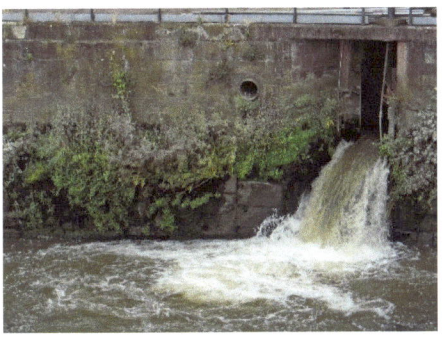

Waterfall by Handbridge, Chester

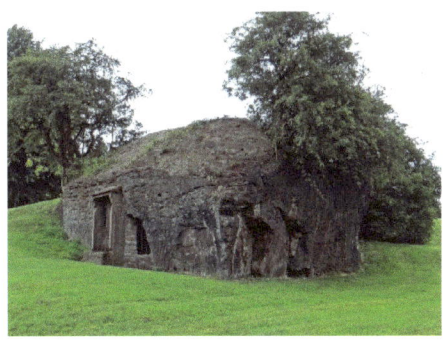

Minerva's Shrine, Chester, Edgar's Field

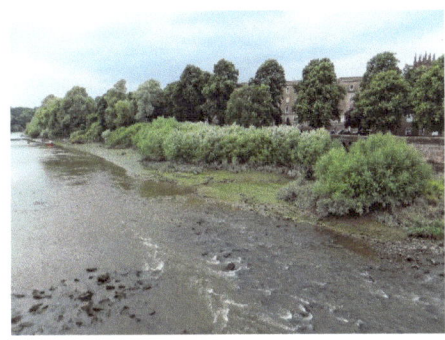

River Dee looking towards University of Chester

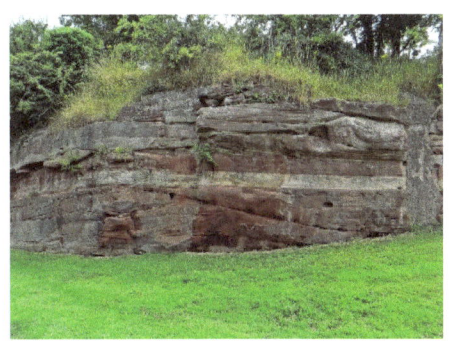

Rock Formation below Minerva's Shrine

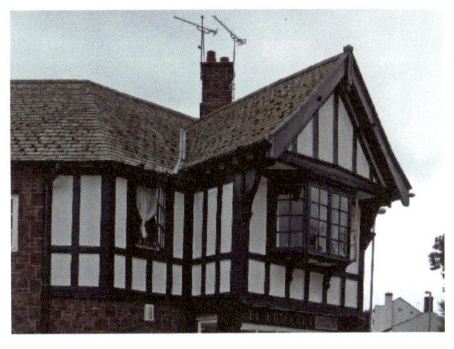

Handbridge Road Architecture

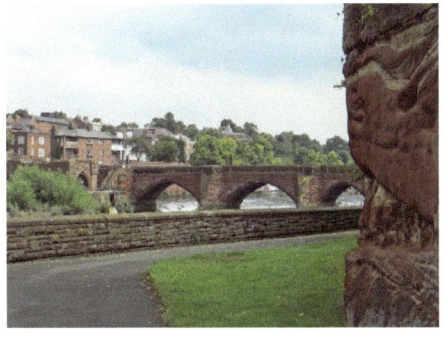

Handbridge, Chester from Edgar's Field

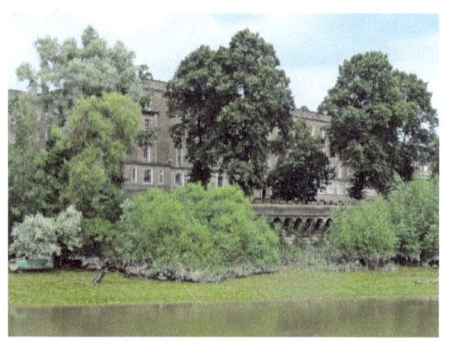

University of Chester

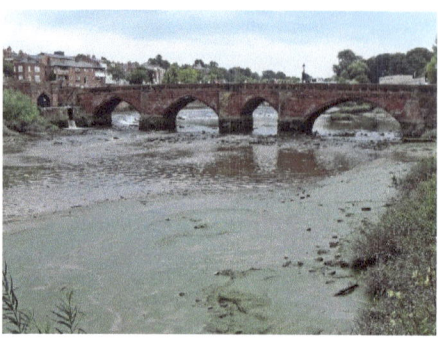

Handbridge

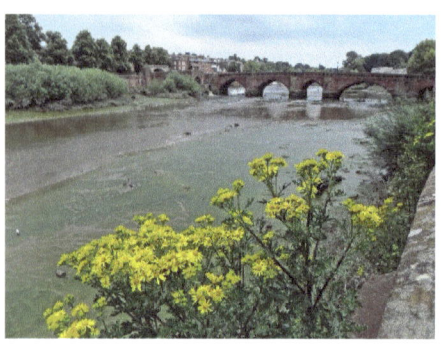

River Dee and Handbridge, Chester

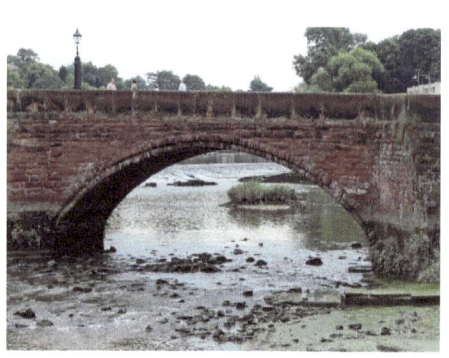

Handbridge Arch

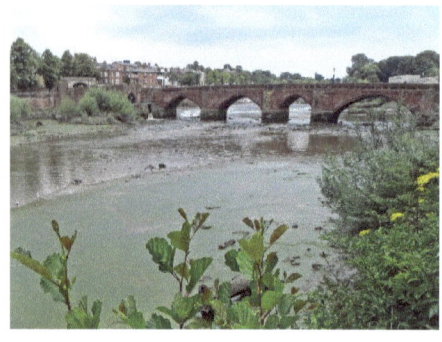

River Dee and Handbridge

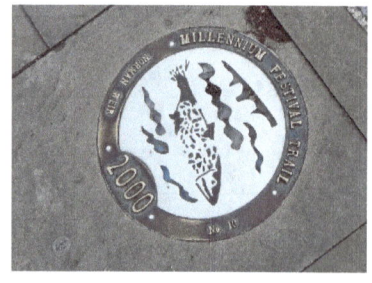

Plaque Norman Weir

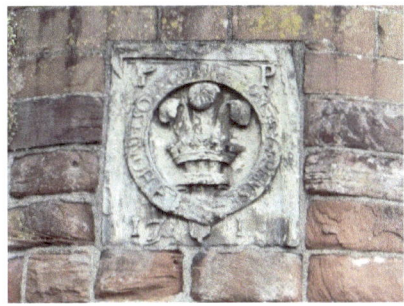

Prince of Wales' Feathers Plaque

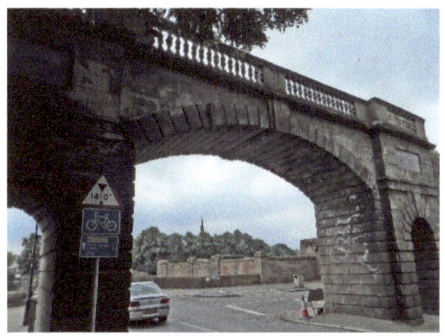

Bridgegate, Chester

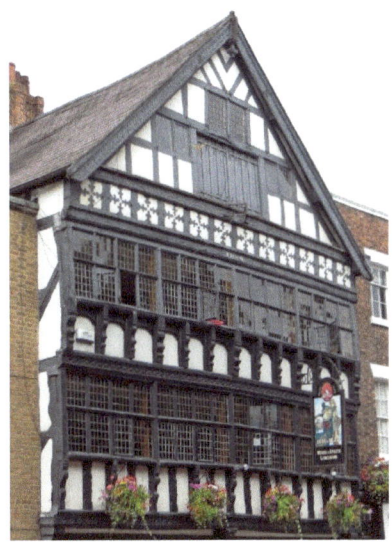

Bear and Billet Pub, Lower Bridge Street, Chester

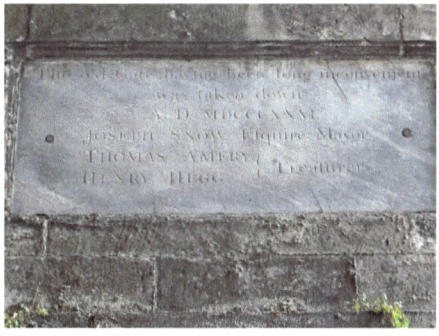

Plaque, Bridgegate, Chester

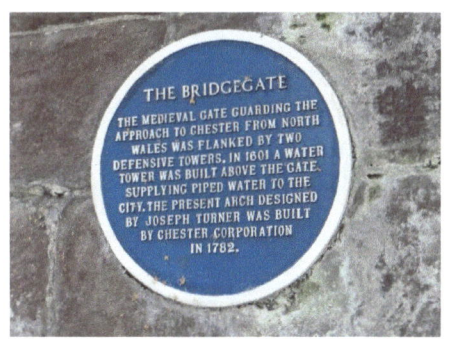

The Bridgegate

Chester A Photographic Glimpse

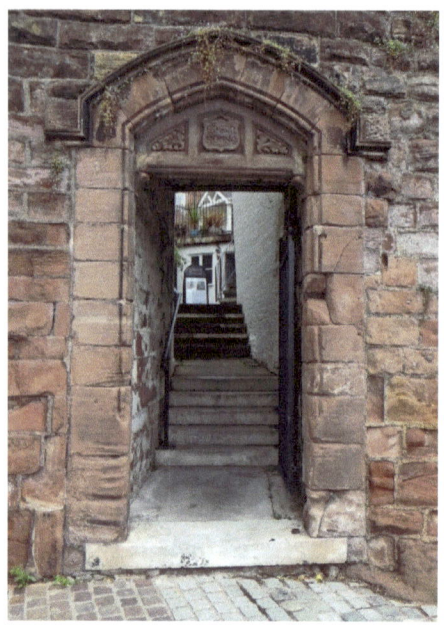

Edgar House, Chester

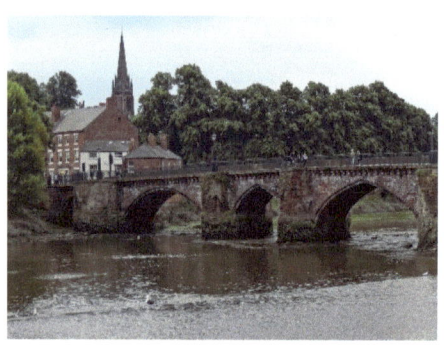

Handbridge Chester Arches

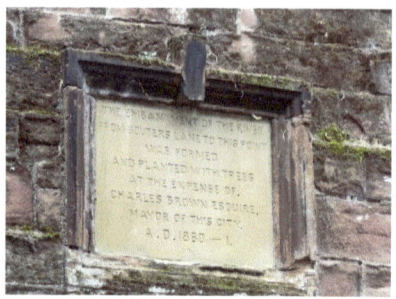

Trees on the embankment of the River Dee

"The Embankment of the River from Souters Land to this Point was formed and planted with trees at the expense of Charles Brown Esquire. Mayor of this City. A.D. 1880 - 1."

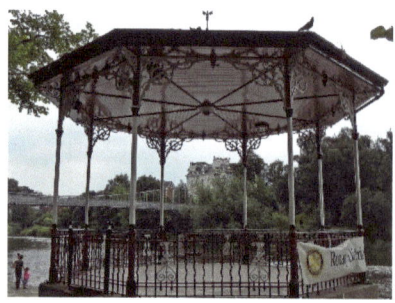

The Bandstand by the River Dee and the Groves

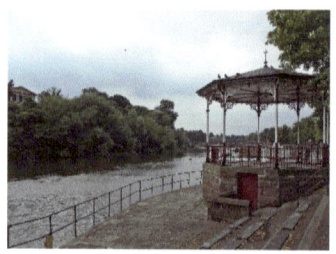

Bandstand by the River Dee and the Groves

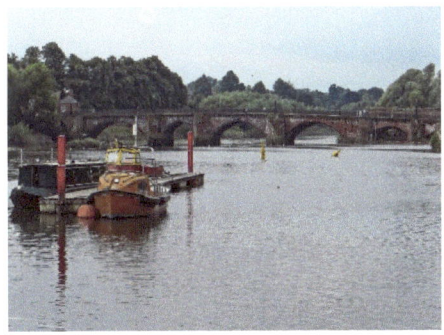

River Dee and Handbridge

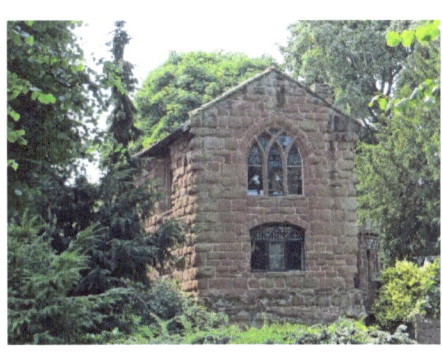

Chester Architecture

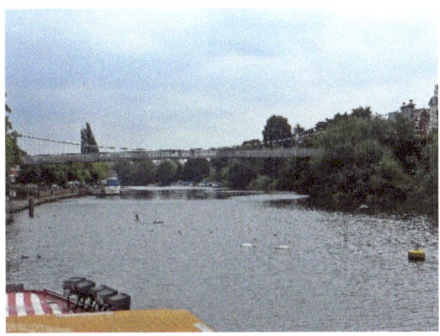

Queen's Park Suspension Bridge, Chester

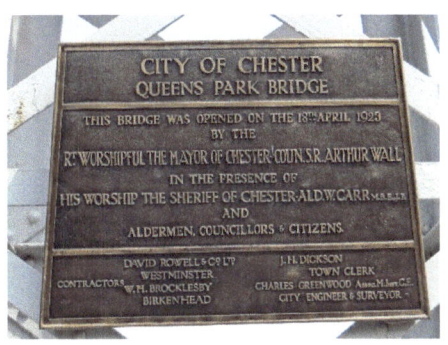

City of Chester Plaque

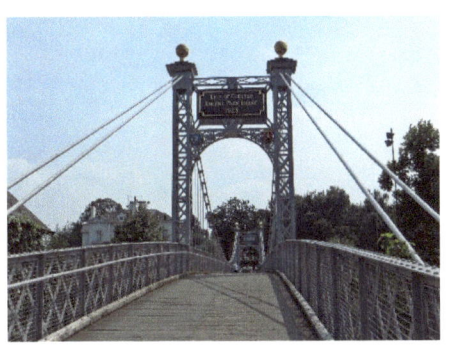

Queen's Park Suspension Bridge City of Chester, 1923

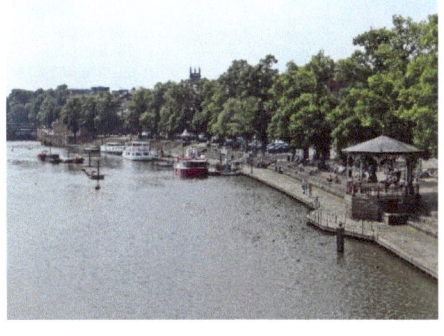

The Groves and Bandstand, Chester

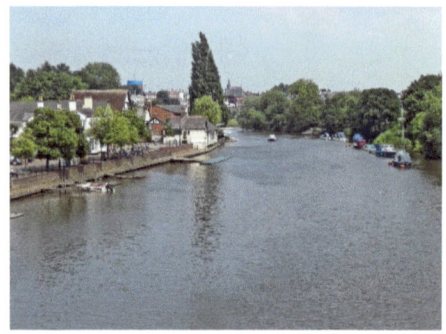
River Dee at Chester

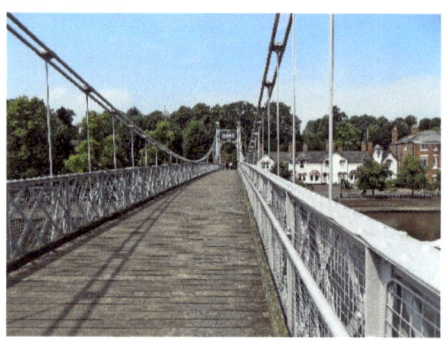
Queen's Park Suspension Bridge Span

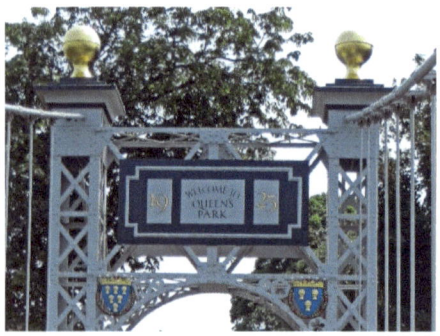
"Welcome To Queen's Park 1923" Signage

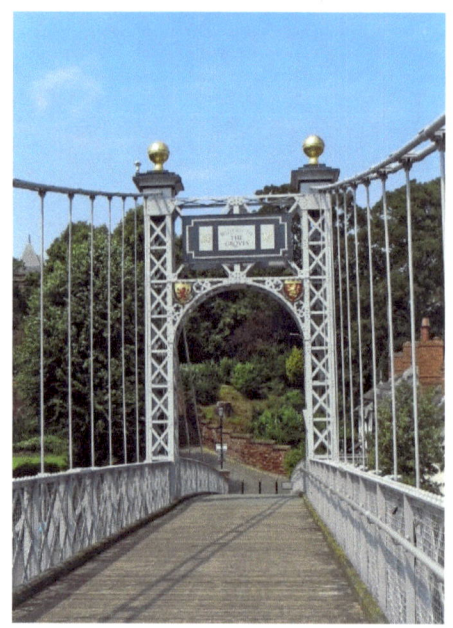
Welcome to the Groves 2012 Plaque

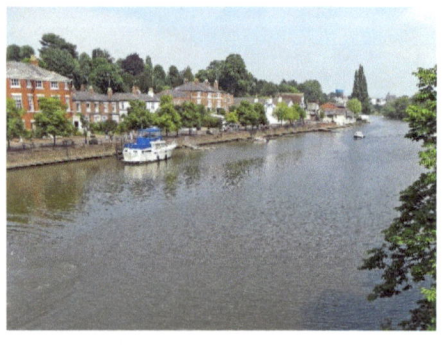
River Dee from Queen's Park, Chester

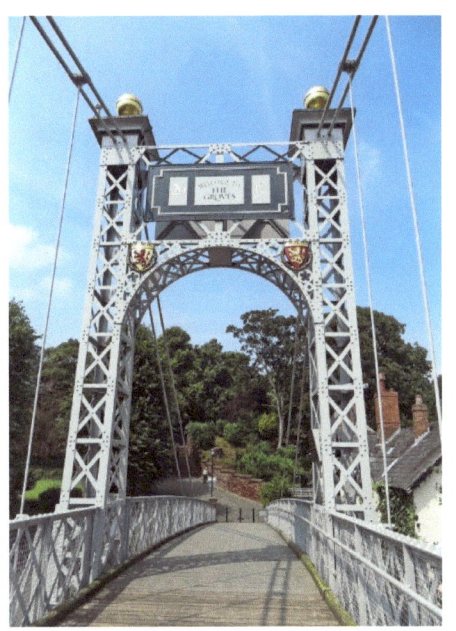

Queen's Park Suspension Bridge Arch

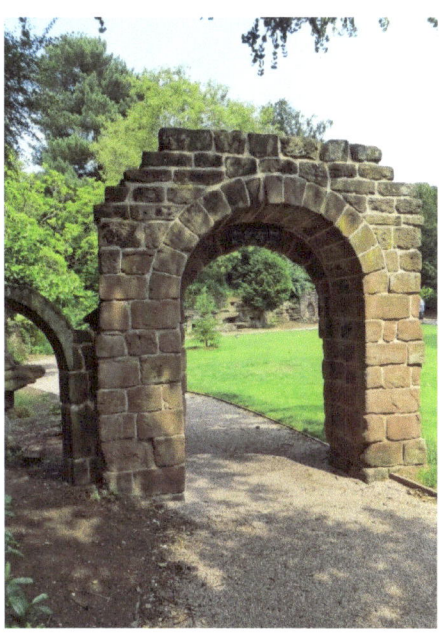

Arch from West Door of Old St. Michael's Church

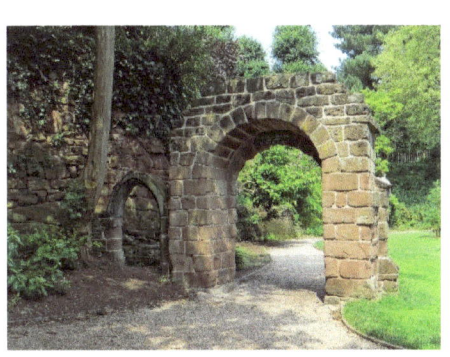

Grosvenor Park, Quarry and Arches from St. Michael's Church, West Door

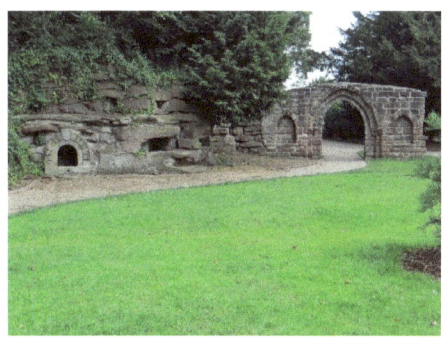

Grosvenor Park Quarry and Arches – Jacob's well and St. Mary's Nunnery Arches

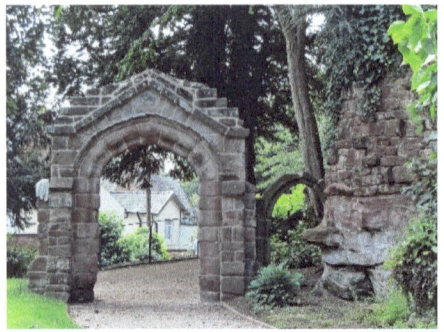

Arch from West Door of Old St. Michael's Church

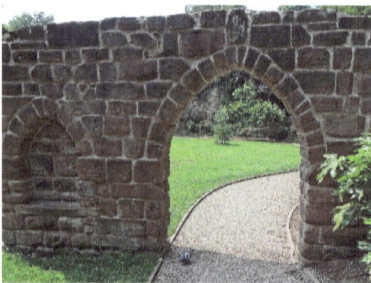

St. Mary's Nunnery Arches Rear View

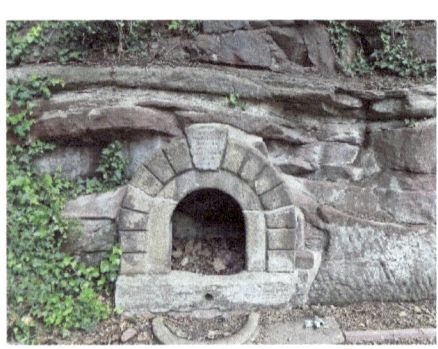

Jacob's Well Arch, Grosvenor Park

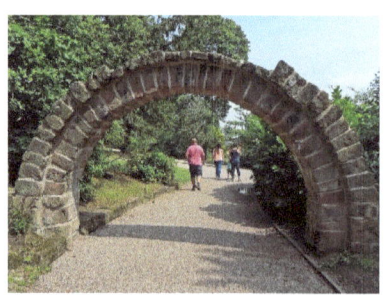

The Old Shipgate Arch, Grosvenor Park, Chester

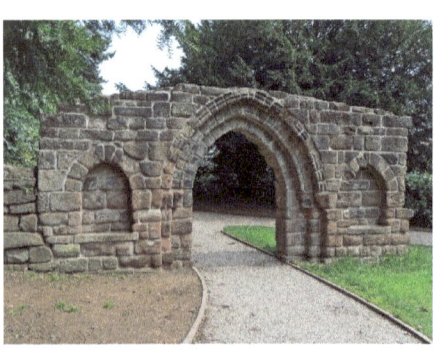

St. Mary's Nunnery Three Arches, Grosvenor Park

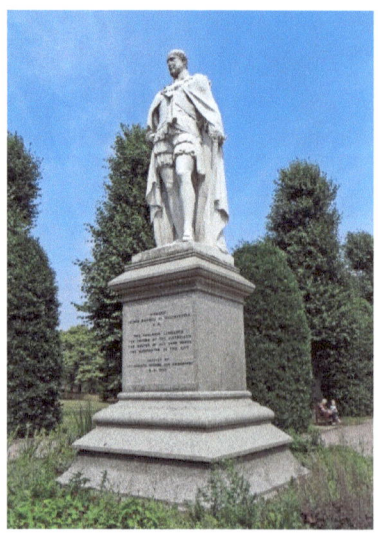

Richard Grosvenor, Stone Statue

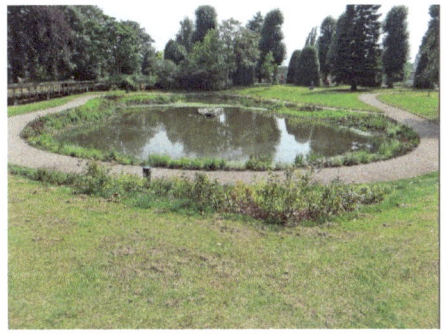
Grosvenor Park Pond, Chester

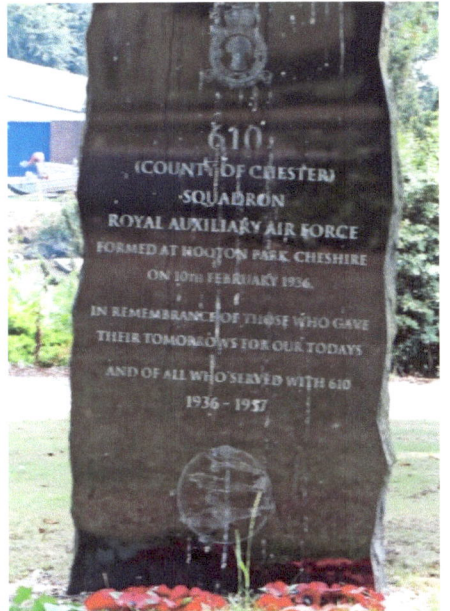
610 Squadron Memorial

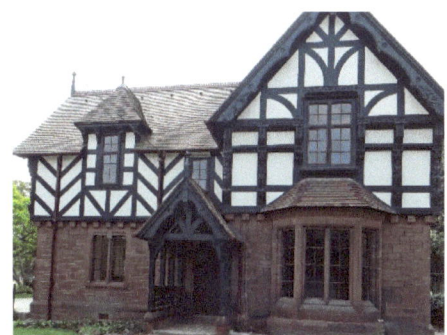
Black & White Modern Architecture

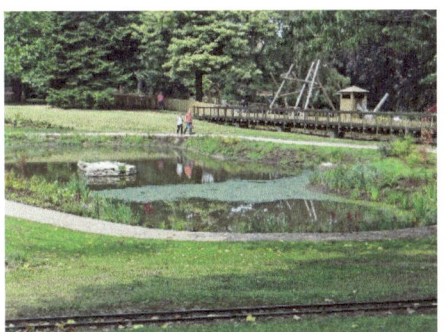
Grosvenor Park Pond, Chester

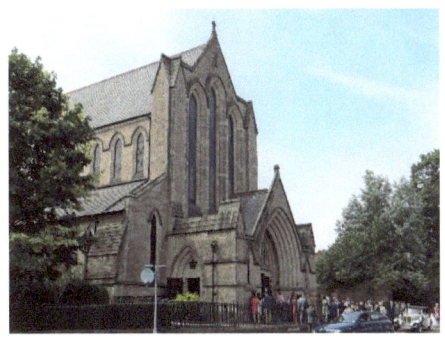
St. Werburgh Church, Chester

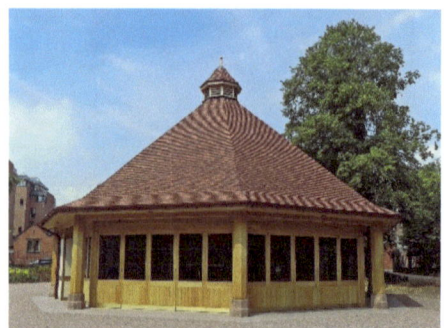

Training Pavilion, Grosvenor Park

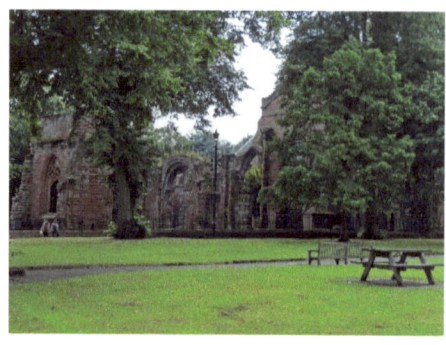

The Church of St. John the Baptist Ruins

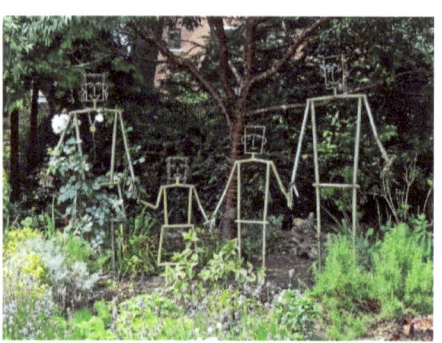

The Family, Grosvenor Park, Chester

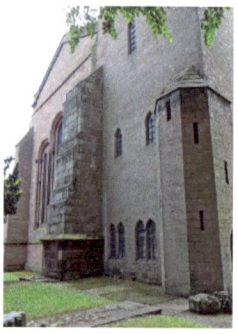

Belfry and Clock Tower, St John's the Baptist Church, Chester

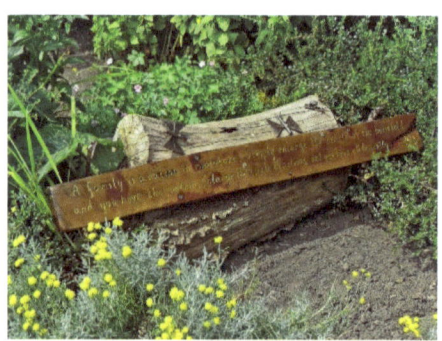

The Family is a nation in miniature

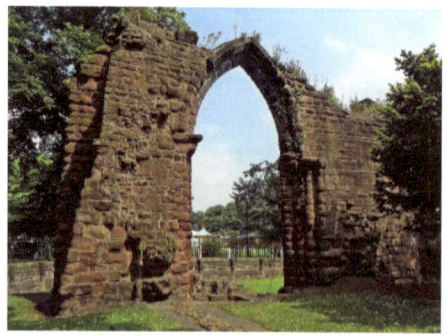

The Church of St. John the Baptist Ruins

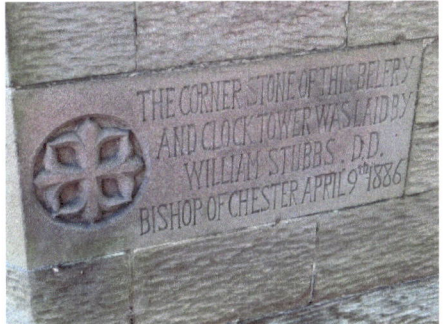
The Corner Stone, St. John the Baptist Church

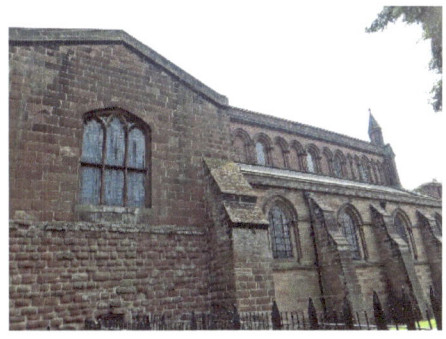
St. John the Baptist Church, Chester - side view

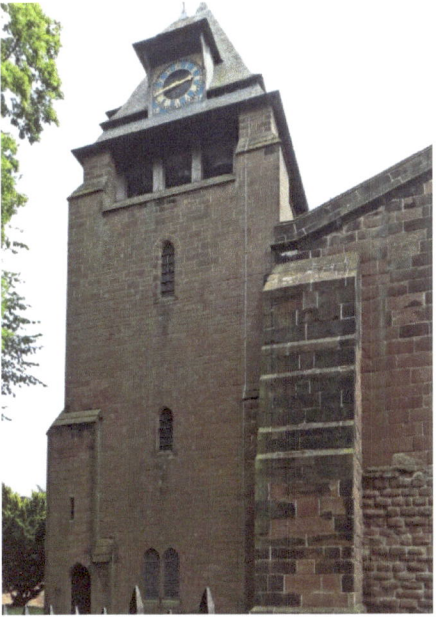
Belfry and Clock Tower, St. John the Baptist Church, Chester

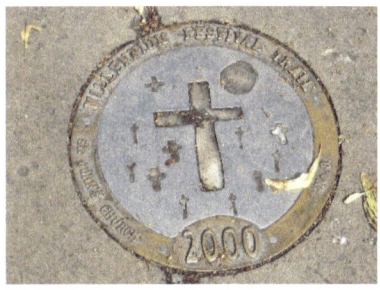
St. John's Church, Millennium Festival Trail Plaque 2000

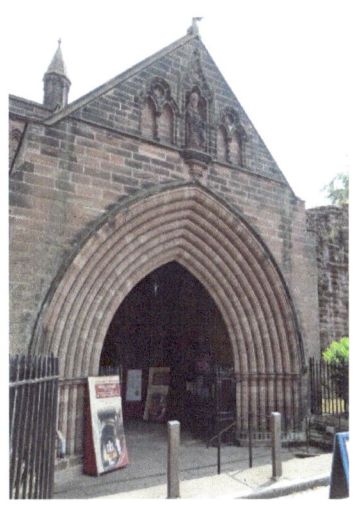
St. John's Church Arched Entrance

Chester A Photographic Glimpse

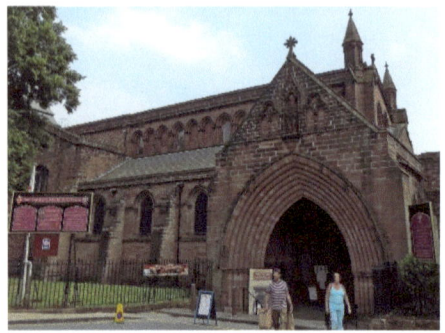

St. John the Baptist Church, Approach, Chester

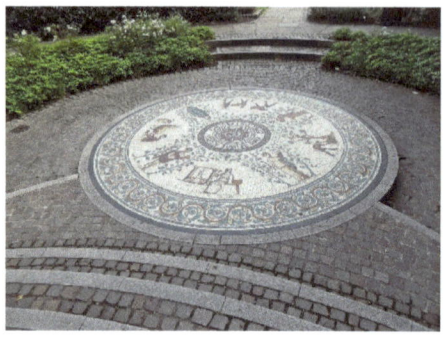

Roman Gardens Mosaic Chester Civil Trust MMX

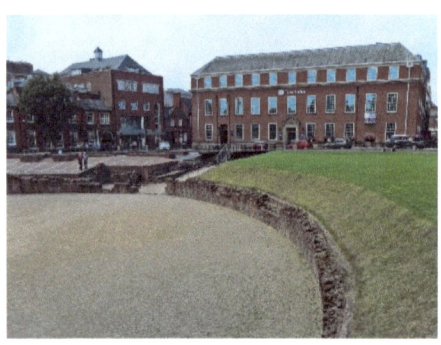

Roman Amphitheatre, Chester

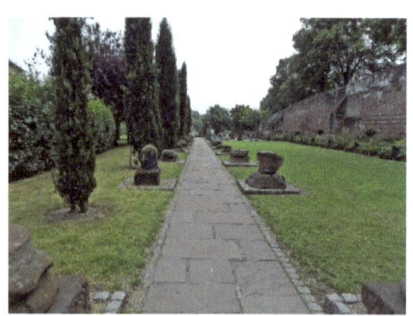

Roman Gardens, Chester

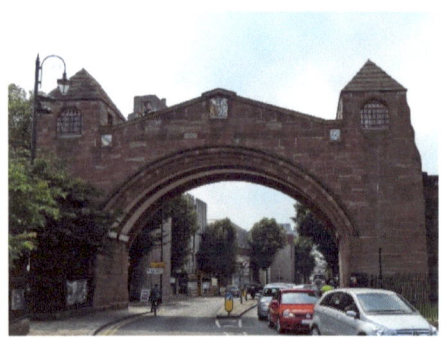

The Newgate, Chester

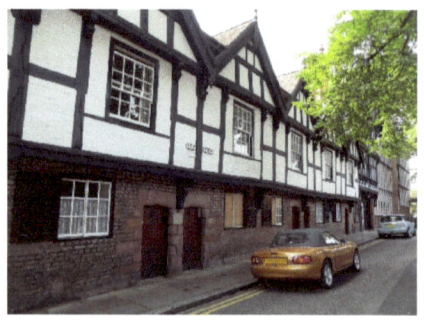

Black and White Buildings, Park Street, Chester

Chester A Photographic Glimpse

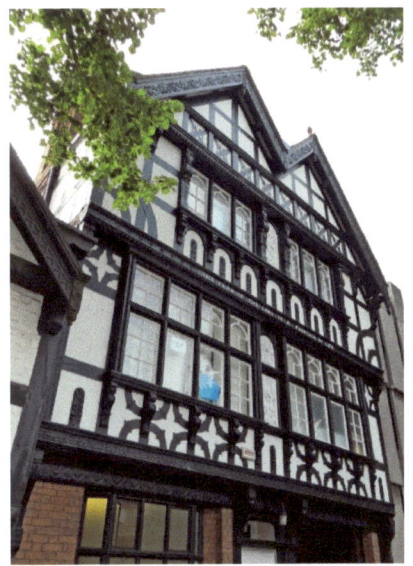

Black and White Architecture, Park Street, Chester

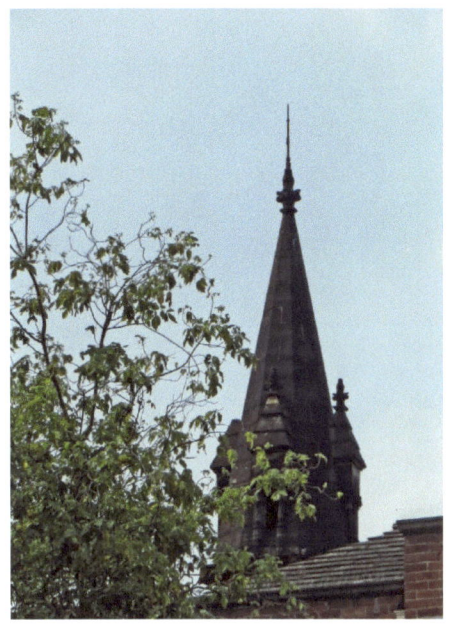

Spire, Chester

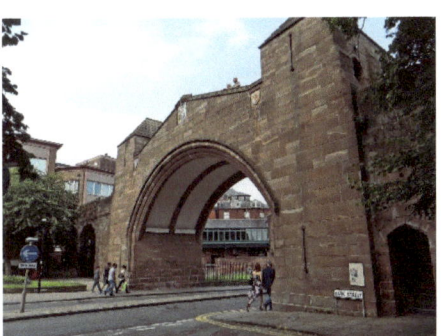

Newgate Bridge, Chester, Steps to City Wall

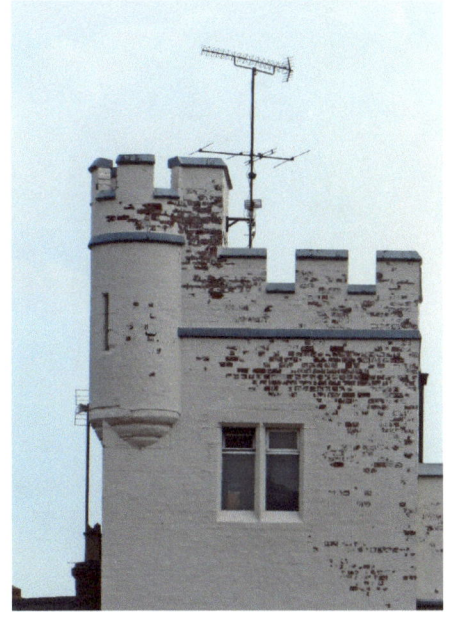

Turret building, Pepper Street, Chester

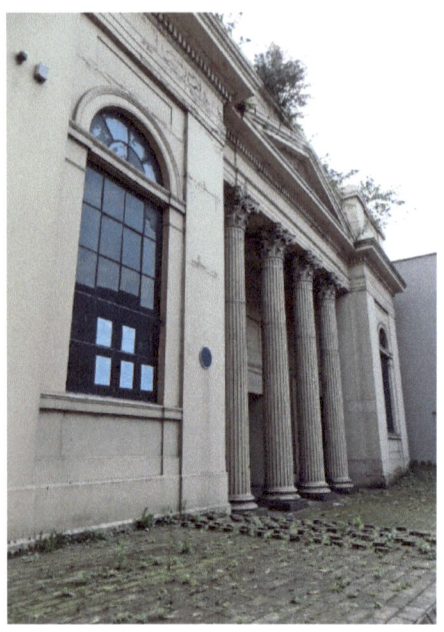

Pepper Street, Chapel, Chester

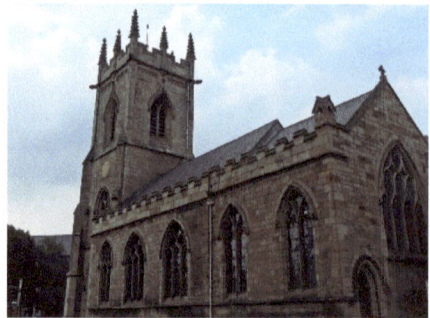

St. Michael's Church, Chester

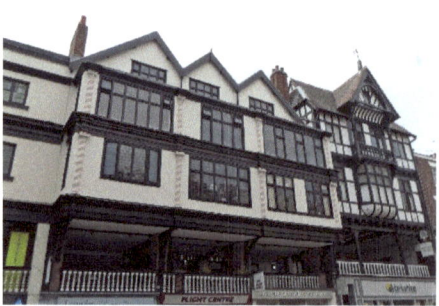

Black & White Revival Architecture

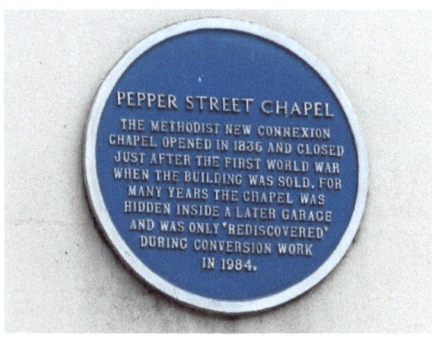

Pepper Street, Chapel, Chester Plaque

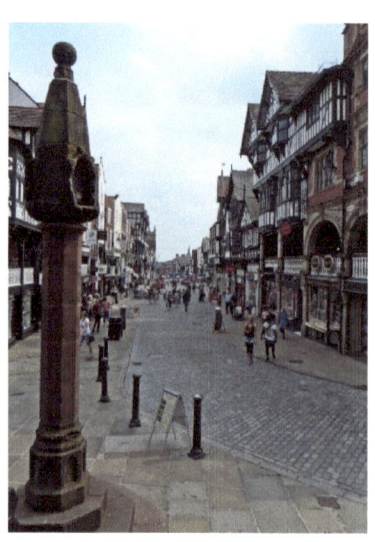

Chester Cross & Bridge Street

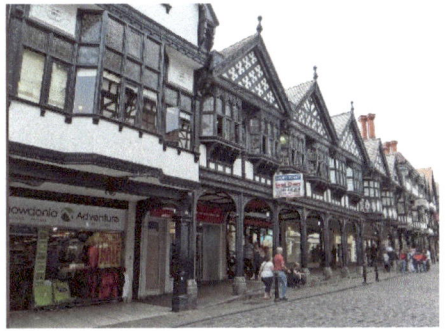

Black & White Revival Architecture, Northgate Street, Chester

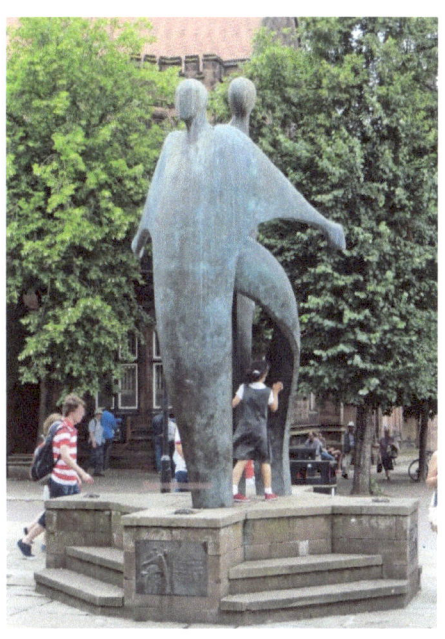

A Celebration of Chester Statue, Northgate Street

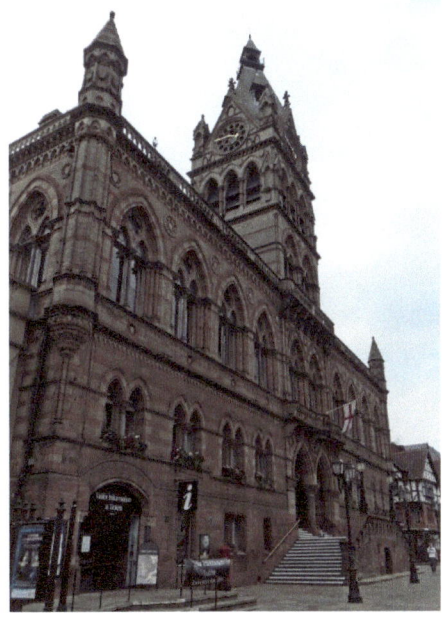

The Town Hall, Chester

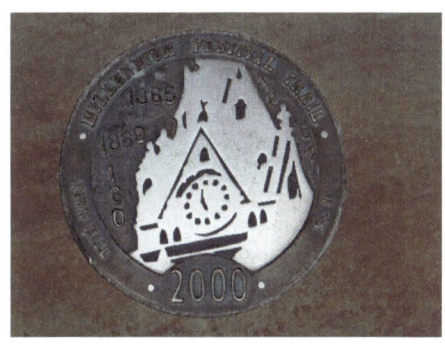

Millennium Festival Trail Town Hall 2000 Plaque

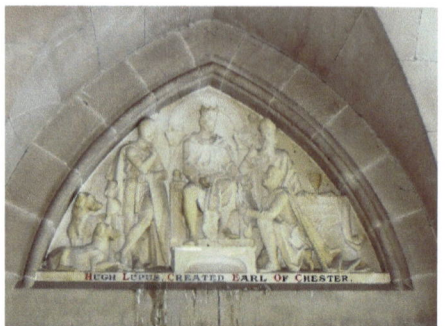

Stone Carving, "Hugh Lupus, Created Earl of Chester"

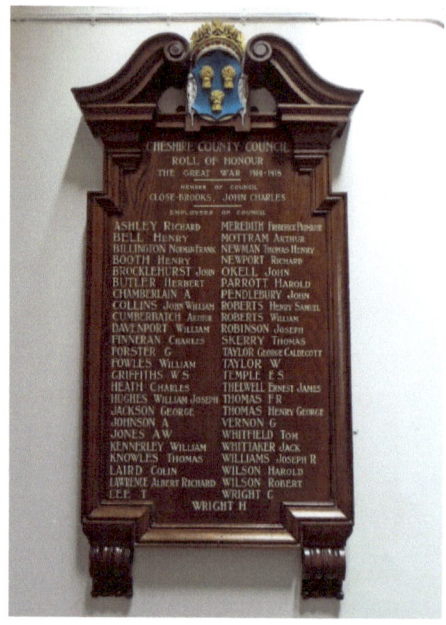

Cheshire County Council Roll of Honour the Great War 1914 - 1918

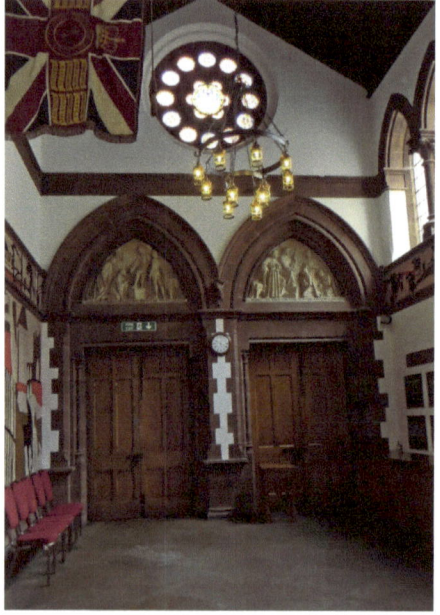

Stone Carvings and Doors, Town Hall, Chester

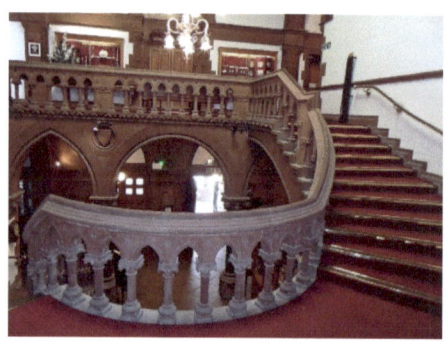

Staircase, Town Hall, Chester

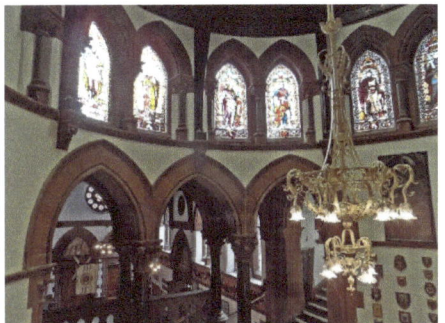

Arches and Stained Glass Windows, Town Hall Chester

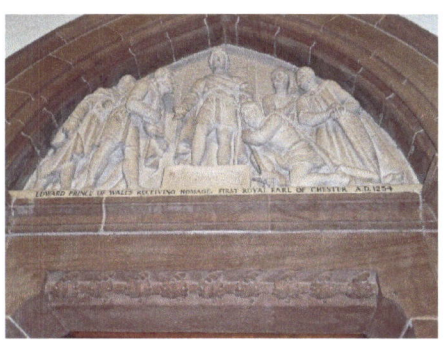

"Edward Prince of Wales Receiving Homage, First Royal Earl of Chester A.D. 1254"

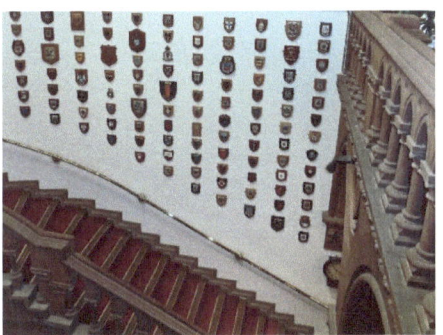

Wall Shields, Town Hall, Chester

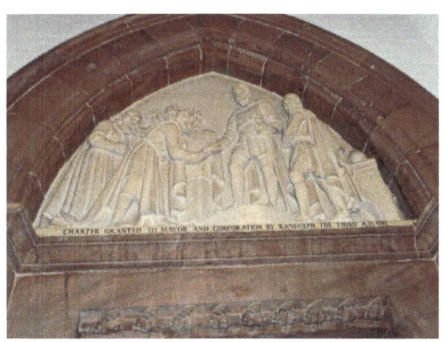

"Charter Granted to Mayor and Corporation by Randolph the Third A.D. 1181", Stone Sculpture, Town Hall

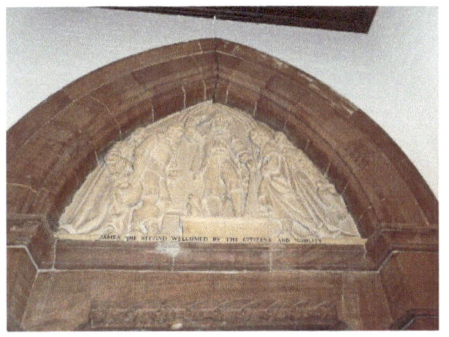

"James the Second Welcomed by the Citizens and Nobility", Stone Sculpture, Town Hall

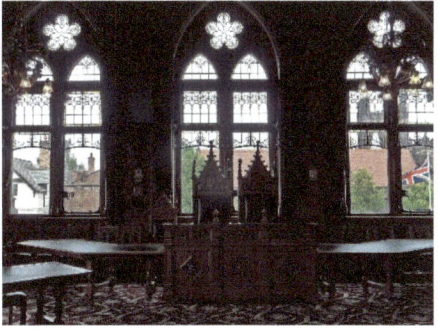

Ornate Chairs and Windows, Town Hall, Chester

Chester A Photographic Glimpse

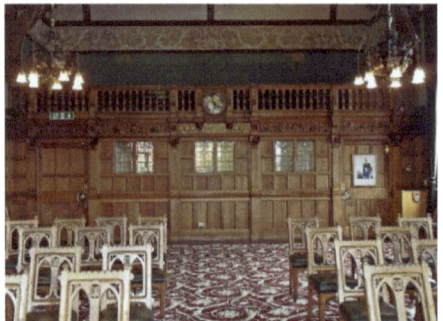

Wooden Balcony, Town Hall, Chester

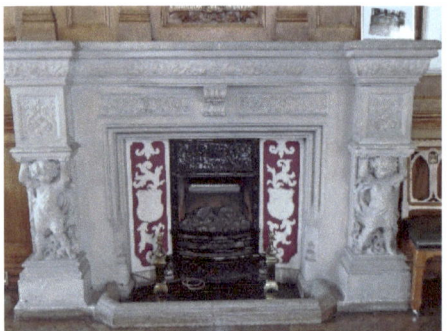

Ornate Fireplace, Town Hall, Chester

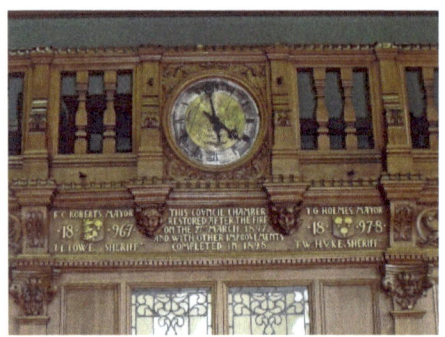

Wooden Balcony and Clock Face and Inscription, Town Hall

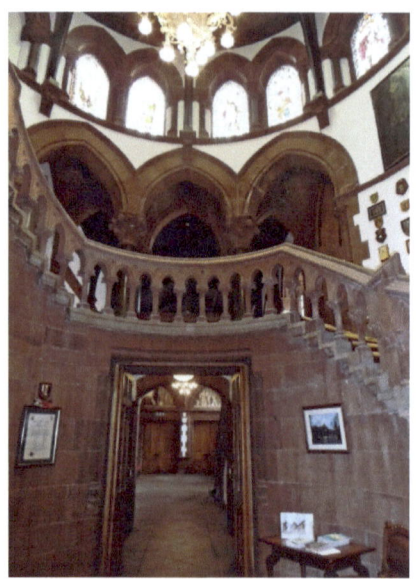

Staircase, looking upward, Town Hall, Chester

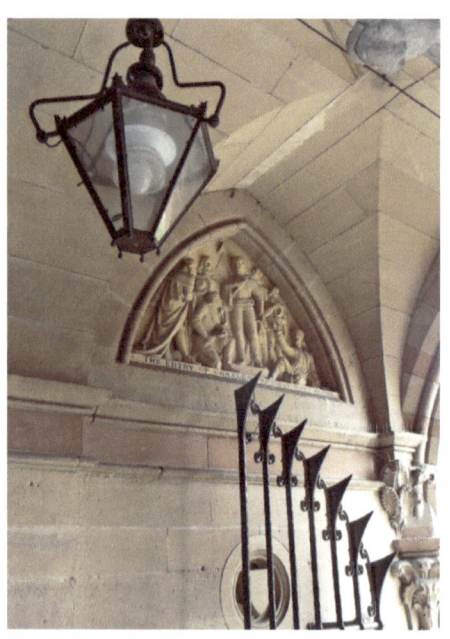

"*The Entry of Charles the First into Chester*", Stone Sculpture, Town Hall

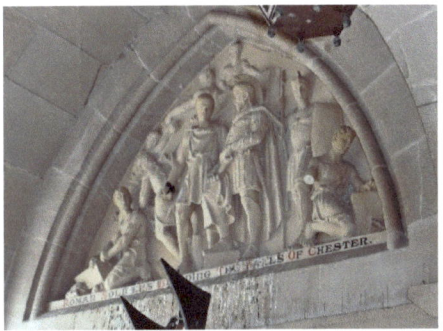

Roman Soldiers Building the Walls of Chester, Stone Sculpture Town Hall

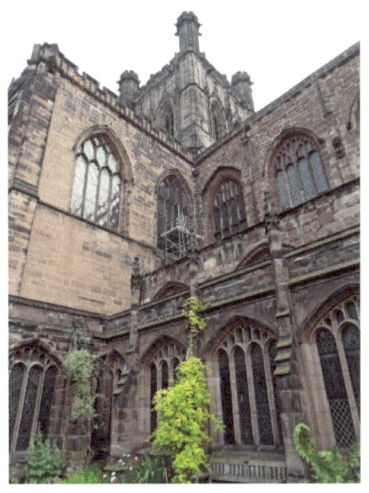

North Tower, Chester Cathedral

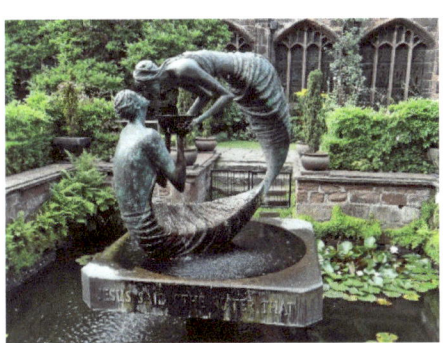

Water Fountain, Chester Cathedral

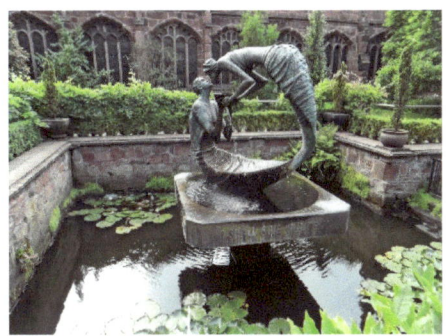

Cloister Garth, with Fountain of Life, Chester Cathedral

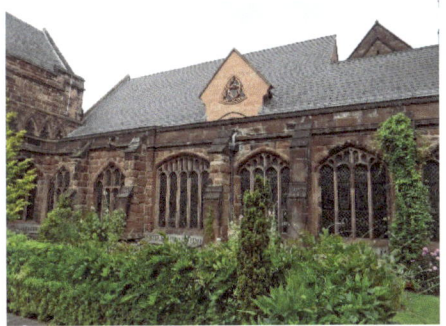

View from Cloister Garth, Chester Cathedral

Chester A Photographic Glimpse

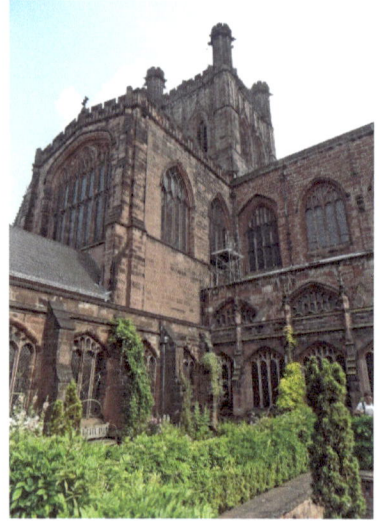

North Tower from Cloister Garth, Chester Cathedral

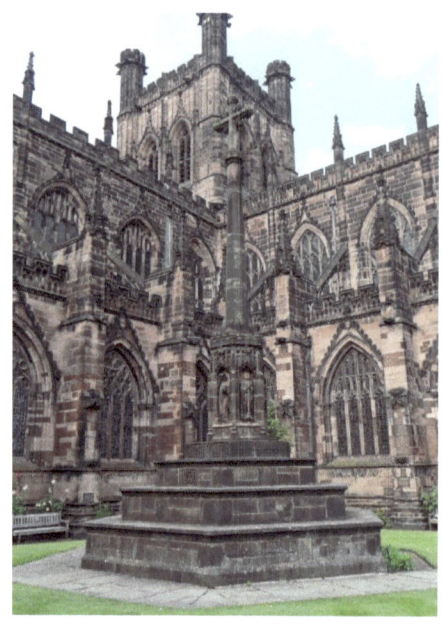

Cross and North Tower, Chester Cathedral

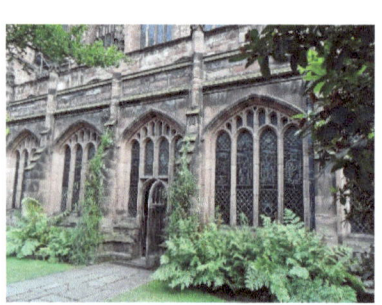

Cloisters, Chester Cathedral

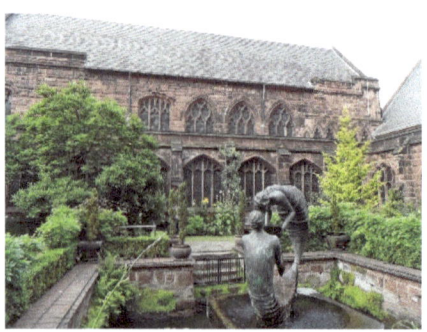

Cloister Garth, with Fountain of Life, Chester Cathedral

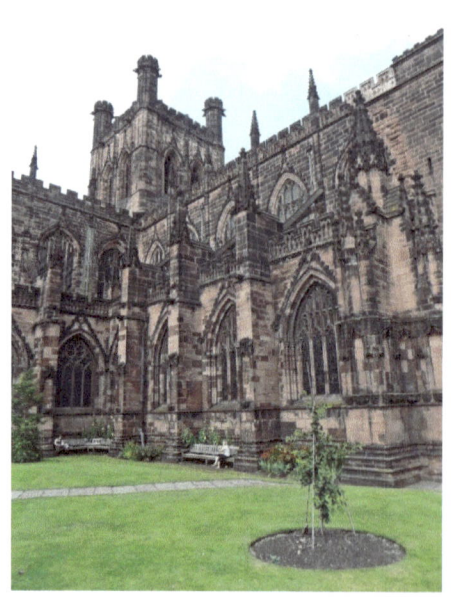

North Tower, Chester Cathedral

Chester A Photographic Glimpse

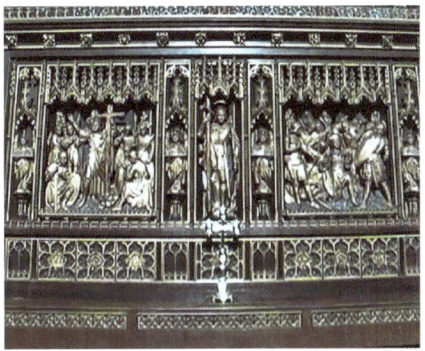

Altar Engravings, Chester Cathedral

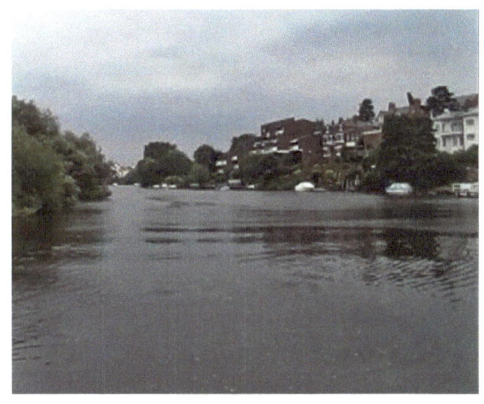

River Dee

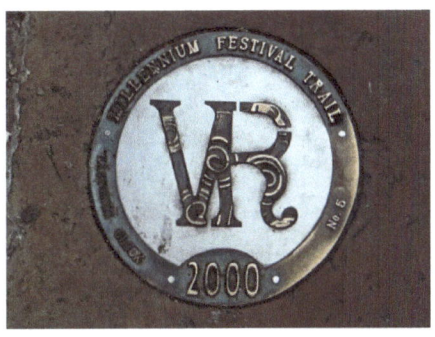

Millennium Festival Trail 2000, East Gate Clock Plaque

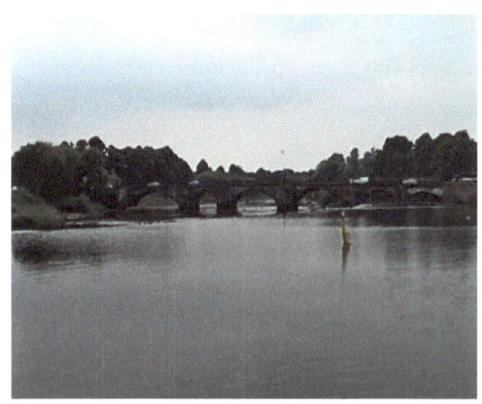

The Old Dee Bridge, Handbridge

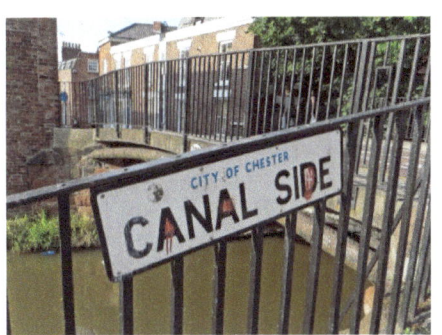

Canal Side, City of Chester

Chester A Photographic Glimpse

Additional Chester Information

This section is prepared for the electronic version of this book and has hyperlinks to photographs. Photographs in the electronic version are of a larger size. The Index in the paperback book version can be used to locate specific images.

Addleshaw Tower

- Addleshaw Tower is free standing;
- Addleshaw Bell Tower of Chester Cathedral;
- Designed by George Pace;
- Foundation stone laid 16 June 1973 by Lord Leverhulme, Lord Lieutenant of Cheshire;
- Bells were installed in 1974;
- 85 feet (26 m) high;
- Known locally as the "*Chester Rocket*";
- Built of sandstone and Welsh slate;
- Plaque, Addleshaw Tower
- Further information, Addleshaw Tower;

Architecture Chester

- Black & White Buildings B&W 1, B&W 2, B&W 3, B&W 4, B&W 5, B&W 6, B&W 7, B&W 8, B&W 9, B&W 10, B&W 11, B&W 12, B&W 13, B&W 14, B&W 15, B&W 16, B&W 17, B&W 18, B&W 19, B&W 20, B&W 21, B&W 22, B&W 23, B&W 24, B&W 25, B&W 26, B&W 27, B&W 28, B&W 29, B&W 30, B&W 31,
- Buildings Architectural Building 1, Architectural Building 2, Architectural Building 3, Architectural Building 4, Architectural Building 5;
- Spire Architecture,
- Black-and-white Revival was an architectural movement from the middle of the 19th century in the Tudor style;
- Built smaller at ground level and extends outwards upward, supported by pillars;

- Buildings were built our on upper storeys to avoid pay tax on ground floor space;
- Ground level is mostly shops, although parts have upper shopping parades;
- Revival Architecture further information;

Bandstand by the River Dee and the Groves;

- Bandstand;
- Bandstand and Groves;
- River Dee Bandstand;
- Chester's Bandstand further information;

Bear and Billett Public House

- Bear and Billet Pub, Lower Bridge Street, Chester;

Bell Tower Walk, Chester

- Architecture, Bell Tower Walk, Chester;

Boot Inn, Chester

- Boot Inn Established 1643;
- Built in the early to middle part of the 17th century;
- Upper storeys are timber-framed with plaster panels with a slate roof;
- Boot Inn, Chester further history;

Bridge Street

- Architecture Bridge Street 1, Bridge Street 2, Bridge Street 3, Bridge Street 4, Bridge Street 5, Bridge Street 6, Bridge Street 1664, Bridge Street Detail
- Bridge Street Art Gallery,
- Bridge Street Modern Architecture,
- Chester Cross looking down Bridge Street1664 Revival Architectural Detail;
- Bridge Street Buildings further history;

Bridgegate, Chester

- Bridgegate;
- Bridgegate Arches, Gothic Arch;
- Plaque, Bridgegate Chester: "*The Old Gate having been long inconvenient was taken down A.D. MDCCLXXX1 Joseph Snow Efquire Mayor Thomas Amery, Henry Hegg Treafurers*", Bridgegate Further History;
- Bridgegate Plaque Blue "*The Bridgegate. The Medieval Gate guarding the approach to Chester from North Wales was flanked by two defensive towers. In 1601 a water tower was built above the gate supplying piped water to the city. The present Arch designed by Joseph Turner was built by Chester Corporation in 1782.*"
- Architect Joseph Turner;
- Built in yellow sandstone ashlar;
- Further history of Bridgegate;

Broughton Water Tower, Chester

- Broughton Water Tower, Chester from the Canal;
- Situated within Chester's water treatment works;

'Celebration of Chester' Statue

- Celebration of Chester Statue;
- Bronze Sculpture by Stephen Broadbent;
- Erected in 1992 partly to commemorate the 300th anniversary of Chester Cathedral;
- Statue in Town Hall Square, Northgate Street;
- Inscription 'A Celebration of Chester', "*Whose City walls make secure the freedom to Work and Worship*";
- Further information, 'Celebration of Chester' Statue;

Chester Canal

- Chester Canal;
- Shropshire Union Canal Main Line;
- Links Nantwich with the River Dee at Chester;
- Opened in 1779;
- Part was closed in 1787, when Beeston locks collapsed;
- Frodsham Street Canal Bridge;
- Canal Side;
- Chemistry Lock, Shropshire Union Canal, Chester; Front View, Chemistry Lock, Sunset at Chemistry Lock
- After the rain, Chester Canal;
- Further information about Chester Canal;

Chester Castle

- 12th Century Agricola Tower, Chester Castle;
- Propylaeum, Chester Castle Designed and built by the architect and engineer Thomas Harrison;
- The Propylaeum, Chester Castle is the ceremonial entrance to the Castle complex;
- Entrance, Chester Castle, Door, Chester Castle;
- Archway, Chester Castle;
- Brickwork and Brickwork and Walls, Chester Castle, Exterior Walls, Chester Castle, Chester Castle, Profile View, Fortifications, Chester Castle, City Wall by Castle;
- Chester Castle's Forecourt;
- Portico, Chester Castle, Chester Castle and Crown Courts, Portico looking Right, Chester Castle;
- Castle Drive Bridge under City Walls Walk, Castle Drive Bridge View;
- Founded by William the Conqueror in 1070;
- The buildings still serve as the county hall, courts and regimental museum;

- The Cheshire Regiment and military finally withdrew in 1999;
- Chester Castle further history;

Chester Cathedral

- Founded in 1092;
- Benedictine Abbey;
- Hugh Lupus, Earl of Chester, Nephew of William I
- Dedicated to St. Werburgh in 1092;
- Closed by Henry VIII as part of the dissolution of the monasteries;
- Made a Cathedral in 1541 by Henry VIII;
- The west front dates from the early 16th century;
- Renovated in the 19th Century by Sir George Gilbert Scott 1868-76;
- Exterior Views Chester Cathedral 1, Chester Cathedral 2, Chester Cathedral 3, Chester Cathedral 4, Chester Cathedral 5, Chester Cathedral 6, Chester Cathedral 7,
- Garden of Remembrance, Chester Cathedral is dedicated to those who lost their lives 1939 – 1945, The Cheshire Regiment;
- G. W. O. Addleshaw Dean 1963 - 1977;
- Statues: Winged Statue, Chester Cathedral;
- Tower & Turrets, Chester Cathedral Weather Vein, Chester Cathedral, North Tower, Chester Cathedral, North Tower from Cloister Garth, Chester Cathedral;
- Water Fountain, Chester Cathedral "The Water of Life" by Stephen Broadbent, Inscription "*Jesus said, the water that I shall give will be an inner spring always welling up for eternal life*." Commissioned by Chester Cathedral and funded by Capital Bank. Dedicated by the Dean of Chester Cathedral, Dr. S. Smalley 8th May 1994;
- Cloister Garth, Chester Cathedral, Cloister View with Fountain of Life, Chester Cathedral, Cloisters,

Chester Cathedral, Cloister Garth and Water of Life Fountain, Chester Cathedral;
- Cross and North Tower, Chester Cathedral;
- Altar Engravings, Chester Cathedral;
- Chester Cathedral's History website, Further history, Chester Cathedral;

Chester City Walls

- Chester City Walls, Adjacent to the Addleshaw Tower;
- Walls walkway Chester City Walls 1 Chester City Walls 2;
- Steps up to Chester City Walls and Chester Cathedral;
- Chester City Walls View from Canal;
- City Walls by Castle;
- The Romans built the City Walls to protect their Roman Fortress Deva;
- Chester was one of the most strongly defended cities; protected by its walls;
- Built from sandstone blocks;
- Chester City Walls by Addleshaw Tower;
- Chester City Walls by River Dee;
- Further information History of Chester City Walls;
- Further Information Walking Chester's City Walls;
- Further Information Walking the Walls, Chester;

Chester Cross

- Chester Cross;
- Chester's Cross looking down Bridge Street;
- A medieval red sandstone cross;
- Cross's history;

Chester's Crown Court

- Chester's Crown Court;
- Forecourt, Chester's Crown Court;

- History of Chester's Crown Court;

Chester Grosvenor Hotel

- Chester Grosvenor Hotel; Chester Grosvenor Hotel, Emblem, Chester Grosvenor Hotel;
- History of Chester's Grosvenor Hotel;

Chester Lions

- Chester Lions Jubilee Bench;
- Inscription: "*Chester Lions Golden Jubilee 2010, Commemorating 50 years service*";
- Adjacent to Chester's Medieval Cross;

Chester Weir

- Chester Weir;
- River Dee at Chester Weir, View of The Groves and Chester Weir;
- Steps in the Chester Weir;
- The weir was built in sandstone in 1093;
- Build for Hugh Lupus and the Benedictine Abbey, Chester Cathedral and Medieval Mills;
- Serves Chester City Council's hydro-electric power station;
- Millennium Festival Trail Norman Weir, 2000 Plaque;
- History of Chester's Weir;

Cheshire County Council

- Plaque, Cheshire County Council: "*Cheshire County Council 1889 - Centenary - 1989 This Plaque which commemorates the Hundredth year of service by the County Council was unveiled by H.R.H. Prince of Wales, Earl of Chester 7 July 1989*";

Chester A Photographic Glimpse

Chester Town Hall

- [Chester's Town Hall front view](#) Elevation;
- Designed by the Belfast architect WH Lynn;
- Built 1865 – 69, at a cost of £40,000;
- Opened by the Prince of Wales in 1869;
- Gothic in style;
- Build of grey and pink sandstone;
- [The Clock Tower, Chester Town Hall](#) is 160 feet high;
- Houses the Lord Mayor's Parlour;
- [Plaque, Chester Town Hall](#);
- [Hugh Lupus Stone Carving, Chester Town Hall](#);
- [Stone Carvings and Doors, Chester Town Hall](#), *"Black Prince Granting Charter To Citizens"* Stone Carving and *"Henry The Seventh Constituting Chester a County"* Stone Carving with Wooden Doors;
- Roll of Honour, Chester Town Hall

    1914 – 1918 Cheshire County Council. [Roll of Honour, Chester Town Hall](#). *"The Great War 1914 - 1918. Member of Council, Close-Brooks, John Charles. Employees of Council.*

    Richard Ashley, Henry Bell, Norman Frank Billington, Henry Booth, John Brocklehurst, Herbert Butler, A chamberlain, John William Collins, Arthur Cumberbatch, William Davenport, Charles Finnerran, G Forster, William Fowles, W S Griffiths, Charles Heath, William Joseph Hughes, George Jackson, A Johnson, A W Jones, William Kennerley, Thomas Knowles, Colin Laird, Albert Richard Lawrence, T Lee, Frederick Primrose Meredith, Arthur Mottram, Thomas Henry Newman, Richard Newport, John Okell, Harold Parrott, John Pendlebury, Henry Samuel Roberts, William Roberts,

Joseph Robinson, Thomas Skerry, George Caldecott Taylor, W Taylor, E S Temple, Ernest James Thelwell, F R Thomas, Henry George Thomas, G Vernon, Tom Whitfield, Jack Whittaker, Joseph R Williams, Harold Wilson, Robert Wilson, C Wright, H Wright."

- Staircase, Chester Town Hall, Staircase looking up, Chester Town Hall;
- Arches and Stained Glass Windows, Chester Town Hall;
- Wall Shields, Chester Town Hall;
- "*James The Second Welcomed by the Citizens and Nobility*" Stone Sculpture, Chester Town Hall;
- "*Edward Prince of Wales Receiving Homage. First Royal Earl of Chester A.D. 1254*" Stone Sculpture, Chester Town Hall;
- "*Charter Granted to Mayor and Corporation by Randolph The Third A.D. 1181*" Stone Sculpture, Chester Town Hall;
- "*The Entry of Charles the First into Chester*" Stone Sculpture, Chester Town Hall;
- "*Roman Soldiers Building the Walls of Chester*" Stone Sculpture, Chester Town Hall;
- Ornate Chairs and Windows, Chester's Town Hall;
- Wooden Balcony, Chester's Town Hall;
- Ornate Fireplace, Chester's Town Hall;
- Clock & Inscription on Wooden Balcony, Chester's Town Hall;
- Chester's Town Hall, further information;

Cheshire Regiment

- Memorial, Cheshire Regiment;
- Military Museum, Cheshire Regiment;
- 22nd Cheshire Regiment Memorial 22nd Cheshire Regiment Memorial inscription;
- 22nd Cheshire Regiment Tercentenary Plaque, Cheshire Regiment; "*The 22nd (Cheshire)*

Regiment 1689 - Tercentenary – 1989. This Plaque, which commemorates the Regiment's long association with its County, was unveiled by H.R.H the Prince of Wales, Earl of Chester 1 July 1989." Situated at the Base of Queen Victoria's Statue, Chester Castle;
- Cheshire Regiment further information;

Cotton, Field Marshal Stapleton, 1st Viscount Combermere GCB, GCH, KSI, PC

- Field Marshal Stapleton Cotton's Equestrian Statue, Profile of Field Marshal Stapleton Cotton's Statue;
- Inscription: - "*Erected in honour of Stapleton Cotton Viscount Combermere Field Marshall: Flanders. Lincelles. The Douro. Talavera. Torres Vedras. Bussaco. Villa Garcia. Llerena. Castrajon. Fuentes De Onoro. Salamanca. Ciudad Rodrigo. El Bodón. The Pyrenees. Orthez. Toulouse.*"
- "*Born 1773 Died 1865*;"
- MP for Newark;
- Equestrian statue was the work of Carlo, Baron Marochetti;
- Biography, Field Marshal Stapleton Cotton;

Dewa Roman Experience

- Dewa Roman Experience,
- Stone Tablet, Dewa Roman Experience,
- Jail, Dewa Roman Experience;

East Gate

- Arch, East Gate, Small Archway, East Gate;
- East Gate, Side View, Arch, East Gate, East Gate 1, East Gate 2, East Gate 3, East Gate 4, East Gate 5, East Gate 6, East Gate 7;

- East Gate Clock is at entrance to the Roman fortress of Deva Victrix constructed in about A.D.74 or A.D.75;
- Sits on a three-arched sandstone structure;
- Forms part of Chester City Walls and can be walked under;
- In 1899 a clock was erected to the top of the gateway in celebration of the Queen Victoria's Diamond Jubilee;
- There is a clock Face on all four sides;
- Designed by John Douglas, a Chester Architect;
- The open wrought ironwork is by James Swindley;
- The clock's faces and mechanism were paid for by Edward Evans-Lloyd, a local solicitor and freeman of the city;
- The clock mechanism was made by J. B. Joyce & Company of Whitchurch, Shropshire in 1897;
- The inscription reads" *This Clock Tower was erected in commemoration of the 60th Year of the reign of Victoria, Queen and Empress*";
- Also on the west side "*Antiqui Colant Antiquum Dierum: B.C. Roberts, Mayor 1897; J.C. Holmes, Mayor 1898*";
- On the south side "*This clock was erected by Edward Evans-Lloyds citizen and Freeman 1897*";
- The north side reads "Erected by public subscription and completed A.D. 1899 H. Stolteforth Mayor";
- In gilt is the date 1897 under each clock face and above "VR". ;
- Above the clock is a copper ogee cupola, surmounted by a weather vane;
- Further information about East Gate and East Gate Clock;

East Gate Street, Chester

- East Gate Street, Chester 1, Grosvenor hotel, East Gate Street, Chester, East Gate Street, Chester 2, East Gate Street, Chester 3, East Gate Street, Chester 4, East Gate Street, Chester 5, East Gate Street, Chester 6, East Gate Street, Chester 7, East Gate Street, Chester 8;
- Chester Grosvenor, East Gate Street;
- East Gate known in Roman times, as the Porta Principalis Sinistra;

Edgar's Field

- Minerva's Shrine, Edgar's Field, Chester;
- Rock Formation Below Minerva's Shrine in Edgar's field;
- Handbridge View from Edgar's Field;
- Further information about Edgar's Field;

Edgar House, Chester

- Edgar House, Chester;
- Edgar House, Chester Website;

Frodsham Street, Chester

- Frodsham Street Canal Bridge;
- Frodsham Street, Chester, Street View, Frodsham Street, Chester 1, Frodsham Street, Chester 2;

Godstall Lane

- Godstall Lane Sign;

Grosvenor

- Grosvenor Shopping Centre, Chester;
- Grosvenor Hotel; Grosvenor Hotel Grosvenor Hotel's Emblem;
- Grosvenor Street Architecture;

- Grosvenor Museum, Chester;

    Grosvenor Museum of Natural History and Archaeology founded in 1885; Exterior Architecture, Grosvenor Museum, Chester;

    Arch details, Grosvenor Museum, Chester;

    Side View, Grosvenor Museum, Chester;

    Clock, Grosvenor Museum, Chester;

    Chimneys, Grosvenor Museum, Chester;

    History of Grosvenor Museum, Chester;

    Plaque, Grosvenor Museum, Chester;

    Foundation Stone, Grosvenor Museum, Chester;

    Staircase, Grosvenor Museum, Chester;

    Mosaic Staircase, Grosvenor Museum, Chester;

- Grosvenor Bridge, Chester Single-span stone arch road bridge; Spans the River Dee; designed by Thomas Harrison: Opened by Princess Victoria of Saxe-Coburg-Saalfeld on 17 October 1832; Grosvenor Bridge history;
- Grosvenor Bridge Model. "*This original model of Thomas Harrison's design for the Grosvenor Bridge was restored and resited here by the Cheshire Civic Trust 1979*";
- Grosvenor Park

    Quarry and Arches, Grosvenor Park;

    Arch from West Door of Old St. Michael's' Church, Grosvenor Park, "*Arch from West door Old St. Michael's Church*" Arch from West door of old St. Michael's Church now situated in Grosvenor Park, Arch from West door Old St. Michael's Church, Grosvenor Park, Chester;

Jacob's Well Arch, Grosvenor Park, Inscription from the New Testament "*Whosoever drinketh of this water shall thirst again*";

St. Mary's Nunnery Arches, Grosvenor Park, St. Mary's Nunnery Arches View, Grosvenor Park;

Shipgate Arch, Grosvenor Park, Chester;

610 Squadron Memorial Grosvenor Park;

Grosvenor Park Pond view toward play area, Pond, Grosvenor Park;

Training Pavilion, Grosvenor Park;

Lodge Cafe, Grosvenor Park;

The Family Sculptures, Grosvenor Park, The Family Quote, Grosvenor Park, "*The Family is a nation in miniature. Simply enlarge the circle of the household, and you have the nation. Enlarge the circle of nations, and you have all humanity.*"

Groves

- The Groves view from Handbridge;
- View of the Groves;
- Bandstand by the River Dee and the Groves;
- Bandstand and the Groves;
- Welcome to The Groves 2012, Plaque;

Guild Church of St Peter at the Cross, Chester

- Guild Church of St. Peter at the Cross, Chester;
- Founded on the site of the Roman Prætorium by Æthelfleda of Mercia in 907;
- Junction of East Gate Street and North Gate Street, Chester;

- Guild Church of St. Peter at the Cross Church, Chester;
- Further Guild Church of St. Peter at the Cross, Chester further history;

Handbridge, Chester

- River Dee, River Dee by Handbridge;
- Handbridge Architecture, River Dee View;
- Arches, Handbridge, Chester, Handbridge Arch, Handbridge Chester Arches;
- Handbridge Buildings, Chester;
- Handbridge Windows, Chester;
- Waterfall by Handbridge, Chester;
- Handbridge Road Architecture;
- View from Edgar's Field of Handbridge, Chester;
- River Dee and Handbridge, Handbridge View, Handbridge Arches View, Span of River Dee and Handbridge;
- Also Known as the Old Dee Bridge, Chester;
- Adjacent to the Chester Weir;
- History of Handbridge;

History and Heritage

- History and Heritage of Chester's Website;

Jacob's Well, Grosvenor Park, Chester

- Jacob's Well, Grosvenor Park;
- Sandstone arch;
- Set into the rock face;
- Drinking fountain with a dish for pets to drink from, but no water supply;
- At the original location it was a working well on The Groves;
- Formerly situated next to the path leading up to St John's Church;
- Moved in 1923;

- Inscription from the New Testament "*Whosoever drinketh of this water shall thirst again*";

Janya

- [Bronze sculpture of baby elephant](#) given by Chester Zoo in 2010;
- Sculptor Annette Yarrow;
- [Janya means Life in Hindi](#);
- Sited opposite Chester's Guildhall;

Lock Keeper Inn, Chester

- [Lock Keeper Inn, Chester](#);
- Adjacent to Chester Canal;
- Adjacent to [Frodsham Street Canal Bridge](#);
- [Lock Keeper Inn's Website](#);

Map of Chester

- [Map](#);

Marlborough Arms

- Marlborough Arms, St. John's Street, Chester;
- [Black and White Revival Architecture](#);

Matthew Henry VDM Cenotaph

- Presbyterian minister, preacher and writer;
- [Inscription, Matthew Henry VDM Cenotaph](#); "*Erected by Public Subscription 1860*" [Cenotaph Inscription, Matthew Henry, Chester](#); "*Born 18th October 1662, died 22nd June 1714*";
- Architect Thomas Harrison;
- Sculptor of the bronze portrait medallion was Matthew Noble;
- Mason was A. McDonald;
- The [Matthew Henry Obelisk](#) is polished granite pointed upright;

- About 5.8 metres in height.
- Further information about the history of the Matthew Henry Obelisk;

Millennium Festival Trail, Chester

- Millennium Festival Trail 2000, Plaque;
- There are 40 buildings on this walking trail;
- Millennium Festival Trail Norman Weir, 2000;
- Millennium Festive Trail Plaque, St. Mary's Church;
- St. John's Church, Millennium Festival Plaque 2000;
- Chosen because they are as outstanding examples of Chester's architectural development over two millennia, from Roman times to the present;
- The route is approximately three miles;
- Further information about the Millennium Festive Trail;

Mill Hotel & Spa Website

- Mill Hotel & Spa;
- Spans the Chester Canal;
- Former Mill & new buildings;
- Mill Hotel And Spa, Lunches and Dinner Canal Cruises;

Military Museum

- Cheshire Regimental Museum, Emblem, Cheshire Regiment Dragon, Cheshire Military Museum;
- 22nd Cheshire Regimen's website;

Minerva's Shrine, Chester

- Minerva's Shrine, Chester
- Minerva's Shrine situated in Edgar's Field;
- Rock formation below Minerva's Shrine in Edgar's field;

- History of Minerva's Shrine;

Newgate Chester

- Newgate , Chester;
- Steps to City Wall at Newgate;
- Constructed of red sandstone;
- Built in 1938;
- Designed by Sir Walter Tapper And Michael Tapper;
- Further history about Newgate, Chester;

North East Tower, City Walls Chester

- King Charles I, Tower, Chester;
- Also known as the Phoenix Tower and Newton Tower;
- Built of red coursed Sandstone;
- 70 feet (21 m) high;
- Semicircular in shape;
- Further information about the North East Tower, Chester;

Northgate Street, Chester

- Black and White Revival Buildings, Northgate Street, Chester;

Owen Jones

- Plaque "*Owen Jones Died 1858, Chester*";

Pepper Street

- Pepper Street Chapel;
- Plaque, Pepper Street Chapel Inscription "*Pepper Street Chapel. The Methodist New Connexion Chapel opened in 1835 and closed just after the First World War when the building was sold. For many Years the Chapel was hidden inside a later*

garage and was only 'rediscovered' during conversion work in 1984."

Prince of Wales' Feathers

- Plaque, Prince of Wales' Feathers;

Queen's Park

- Suspension Bridge, Queen's Park, Queen's Park Suspension Bridge Span;
- Queen's Park Suspension Bridge Plaque;
- Queen's Park Suspension Bridge. City of Chester, 1923 *"City of Chester. Queen's Park Bridge. this bridge was opened on the 18th April 1923 by the Right Worshipful the Mayor of Chester - Councillor S.R. Arthur Wall in the presence of his worship the Sheriff of Chester- Alderman W. Carr M.B.E. J.P. and Aldermen, Councillors & citizens. David Rowell & Co Limited Westminster. J.H. Dickson Town Clerk. Contractors W. H. Brocklesby Birkenhead. Charles Greenwood Associate Mechanical Institute. C.E., City Engineer and Surveyor."*
- "Welcome To Queen's Park 1923" Signage;
- Queen's Park Suspension Bridge Arch;
- This pedestrian suspension bridge was opened on 18 April 1923;
- The current bridge replaced an earlier Victorian bridge built in 1852;

Queen Victoria's Statue

- Queen Victoria holding the Orb and Sceptre, Statue, Chester Castle;
- Queen Victoria's Bronze Statue, situated in the courtyard of Chester's Castle;
- Plinth Crests on Queen Victoria's Statue;
- Unveiled 1903;
- Sculpted by Frederick William Pomeroy;

- The designer of the stonework was Harry Beswick;
- The stonemasons were Haswell and Sons;
- The pedestal is of Stancliffe stone and has a base of granite;
- Inscription: "*This statue was erected in honour of a good and beloved Queen in grateful remembrance of her long and glorious reign by her Majesty's loyal subjects in the County and City of Chester A.D. 1903.*"
- 22nd Cheshire Regiment Plaque; "*The 22nd (Cheshire) Regiment 1689 - Tercentenary – 1989. This Plaque, which commemorates the Regiment's long association with its County, was unveiled by H.R.H the Prince of Wales, Earl of Chester 7 July 1989.*"
- Cheshire County Council Plaque: "*Cheshire County Council 1889 - Centenary - 1989 This Plaque which commemorates the Hundredth year of service by the County Council was unveiled by H.R.H. Prince of Wales, Earl of Chester 7 July 1989*".
- Further history about Queen Victoria's Statue, Chester;

Richard Grosvenor, 2nd Marquis of Westminster

- Richard Grosvenor, 2nd Marquis of Westminster, Statue, Grosvenor Park, Chester: *Inscription "Richard Second Marquis of Westminster K.C. The generous Landlord; The Friend of the Distressed; The helper of all good works; The Benefactor to this City; Erected by his Tenant Friends and Neighbours A.D. 1869."* Wearing Garter Robes;
- 27 January 1795 – 31 October 1869;
- English politician, landowner, property developer and benefactor;
- Designed by Thomas Thornycroft:
- Erected in 1869;

- Further history of Richard Grosvenor, 2nd Marquis of Westminster's Statue;

River Dee

- River Dee;
- River Dee by Handbridge, ;
- Rock Formation, adjacent River Dee;
- City Walls along by River Dee;
- River Dee at Chester;
- River Boats, River Dee, Chester;
- Tree row by River Dee towards Edgar's Field, Chester;
- Chester Weir;
- River Dee at River Dee at Chester Weir;
- River Dee looking towards University of Chester;
- River Dee and Handbridge, Handbridge View, Span of River Dee and Handbridge;
- Embankment Trees Plaque, River Dee, Chester;
- Queen's Park Pedestrian Suspension Bridge over the River Dee;
- River Dee from Queen's Park, Chester;
- Old Dee Bridge, Chester;
- Further information about the River Dee;

Rock Formation

- Below Minerva's Shrine in Edgar's field;

Roman Amphitheatre, Chester

- Roman Amphitheatre, Chester;
- Excavated in 1929 and 1960, and 2004 to 2006;
- Excavated by Professor Robert Newstead, (1859 - 1947);
- The largest and most elaborate Amphitheatre in Britain;
- Could seat around 7,000 spectators;
- The Arena had four entrances;

Roman Gardens

- Roman Gardens Mosaic: "*Chester Civic Trust. Golden Jubilee MMX*", Based on Mosaic form North Africa, four figures representing the four seasons,
- Roman Gardens;
- Laid out in 1949;
- Constructed from relics found nearby in Chester;

Saddle Inn, Chester

- Saddle Inn, Chester
- Saddle Inn's Website;

Shields

- Wall Shields, Chester – three Barley Sheaves, three Lions;

Shipgate Arch, Grosvenor Park, Chester

- Called the Old Shipgate Arch, Grosvenor Park, Chester;
- The arch once spanned the medieval Shipgate in the City Wall;
- Was located to the west of the present Bridgegate and adjacent to Chester University;
- Moved around 1828 from the City Wall to Abbey Square;
- Placed in the Groves in August 1897;
- Since 1923 located in Grosvenor Park;

St. Francis of Assisi

- St. Francis of Assisi, Catholic Church, Chester;
- St. Francis of Assisi, Church Website;

St. John's the Baptist Church, Chester

- Ruins, St. John's the Baptist Church, Chester;

- Arch, St. John's the Baptist Church, Chester Arched Entrance, St. John's the Baptist Church, Chester, Approach, St. John's the Baptist Church, Chester;
- Belfry And Clock Tower, St. John's the Baptist Church, Chester, Clock Tower, St. John's the Baptist Church, Chester;
- Cornerstone, St. John's the Baptist Church, Chester Inscription: "*The Corner Stone of this Belfry and Clock Tower was laid by William Stubbs. D.D. Bishop of Chester April 9th 1886*";
- St. John's the Baptist Church, Chester, side view;
- St. John's Church Millennium Plaque;
- Chester's oldest Church, founded in 689 by AEthelred, King of Mercia ;
- A site of worship for over thirteen Centuries;
- Ruins stood for over 900 years;
- Further history about St. John's the Baptist Church, Chester;

St. Mary's Church, Chester

- St. Mary's Church's Tower, Chester, behind the University of Chester's entrance;
- Profile view of Tower, St. Mary's Church, Chester, Front Aspect, St. Mary's Church, Chester, Tower, St. Mary's Church, Chester;
- St. Mary's Church Millennium Festival Trail Plaque;
- Formerly Church of St Mary-on-the-Hill, Chester;
- Built in 14th and 15th centuries to serve the Castle;
- Build of red Sandstone;
- Further history of St. Mary's Church, Chester;

St. Mary's Nunnery

- Red Sandstone Arch, Grosvenor Park, Chester from St. Mary's Nunnery;
- St. Mary's Nunnery Arch has winged walls;
- Originally part of St. Mary's Benedictine Nunnery;

- Dates from the 13th Century;
- Originally situated in the West of the City of Chester and established in the 12th century;
- Laid to waste during the dissolution of the monasteries in 1540;
- Relocated in about 1840 and then to Grosvenor Park, possibly around 1871;

St. Michael's Church, Chester

- [History & Heritage](#) at St. Michael's Church, Chester;
- [St. Michael's Church History](#);
- [St. Michael's Arch from West Door of Old St. Michael's' Church](#);
- "*Arch from West Door, Old St. Michael's Church*" [Arch from St. Michael's Church, Grosvenor Park, Chester](#);
- This is a red sandstone arch with an adjacent smaller arch;
- The arch is from the former west door of St. Michael's Church;
- [St Michael's Church](#) stands on the junction of Bridge Street and Pepper Street;
- In 1840 the Church was declared unsafe;
- It was almost totally rebuilt by James Harrison and it is thought the West Door Archway was removed and then relocated in Grosvenor Park;
- [History and heritage website](#);

St. Peter at the Cross Church, Chester

- [St. Peter at the Cross, Chester](#);
- [St. Peter at the Cross Church, Chester](#) view from Bridge Street;
- [Clock Tower, St. Peter at the Cross, Chester](#);

St. Werburgh Church, Chester

- St. Werburgh Church, Chester, Roman Catholic Parish Church;
- Built in the 1870s by Edmund Kirby;
- History of St. Werburgh's Church;

St. Werburgh Street, Chester

- Architecture St Werburgh Street, Chester 1, St Werburgh Street, Chester 2, St Werburgh Street, Chester 3, St Werburgh Street, Chester 4, St Werburgh Street, Chester 5, St Werburgh Street, Chester 6;

Steam Mill, Chester

- Tower, Steam Mill, Chester;
- Business Centre Offices, Steam Mill, Chester;

Temple Bar

- Temple Bar Architecture;

Town Hall, Chester

- Chester's Town Hall front view Elevation;
- Designed by the Belfast architect WH Lynn;
- Built 1865 – 69, at a cost of £40,000;
- Opened by the Prince of Wales in 1869;
- Gothic in style;
- Build of grey and pink sandstone;
- The Clock Tower, Chester Town Hall is 160 feet high;
- Houses the Lord Mayor's Parlour;
- Plaque, Chester Town Hall;
- Hugh Lupus Stone Carving, Chester Town Hall;
- Stone Carvings and Doors, Chester Town Hall, *"Black Prince Granting Charter To Citizens"* Stone Carving and *"Henry The Seventh Constituting*

Chester a County" Stone Carving with Wooden Doors;
- Roll of Honour, Chester Town Hall

    1914 – 1918 Cheshire County Council. Roll of Honour, Chester Town Hall. "*The Great War 1914 - 1918. Member of Council, Close-Brooks, John Charles. Employees of Council.*

    Richard Ashley, Henry Bell, Norman Frank Billington, Henry Booth, John Brocklehurst, Herbert Butler, A chamberlain, John William Collins, Arthur Cumberbatch, William Davenport, Charles Finnerran, G Forster, William Fowles, W S Griffiths, Charles Heath, William Joseph Hughes, George Jackson, A Johnson, A W Jones, William Kennerley, Thomas Knowles, Colin Laird, Albert Richard Lawrence, T Lee, Frederick Primrose Meredith, Arthur Mottram, Thomas Henry Newman, Richard Newport, John Okell, Harold Parrott, John Pendlebury, Henry Samuel Roberts, William Roberts, Joseph Robinson, Thomas Skerry, George Caldecott Taylor, W Taylor, E S Temple, Ernest James Thelwell, F R Thomas, Henry George Thomas, G Vernon, Tom Whitfield, Jack Whittaker, Joseph R Williams, Harold Wilson, Robert Wilson, C Wright, H Wright."
- Staircase, Chester Town Hall, Staircase looking up, Chester Town Hall;
- Arches and Stained Glass Windows, Chester Town Hall;
- Wall Shields, Chester Town Hall;
- "*James The Second Welcomed by the Citizens and Nobility*" Stone Sculpture, Chester Town Hall;
- "*Edward Prince of Wales Receiving Homage. First Royal Earl of Chester A.D. 1254*" Stone Sculpture, Chester Town Hall;

- "*Charter Granted to Mayor and Corporation by Randolph The Third A.D. 1181*" Stone Sculpture, Chester Town Hall;
- "*The Entry of Charles the First into Chester*" Stone Sculpture, Chester Town Hall;
- "*Roman Soldiers Building the Walls of Chester*" Stone Sculpture, Chester Town Hall;
- Ornate Chairs and Windows, Chester's Town Hall;
- Wooden Balcony, Chester's Town Hall;
- Ornate Fireplace, Chester's Town Hall;
- Clock & Inscription on Wooden Balcony, Chester's Town Hall;
- Chester's Town Hall, further information;

University of Chester

- Entrance, University of Chester, Portico, University of Chester;
- Forecourt, University of Chester;
- Modern Front Entrance, University of Chester;
- University of Chester, View From Edgar's Field;
- River Dee looking towards University of Chester;
- University of Chester's website;

Welsh Presbyterian Church, Chester

- Welsh Presbyterian Church, St. John's Street, Chester;
- Built in 1866;
- Designed by W. & G. Audsley;
- Built of yellow sandstone;
- Sign in Welsh, Welsh Presbyterian Church, Chester;

610 Squadron

- 610 Squadron Memorial Grosvenor Park, Chester;
- Inscription: *"610 (County of Chester) Squadron; Royal Auxiliary Air Force; Formed at Hooton Park,*

Cheshire on 10th February 1936. In remembrance of those who gave their tomorrows for our todays and all who served with 610; 1936 – 1957";

- [610 Squadron Memorial, Grosvenor Park, Chester, history](#);

Chester A Photographic Glimpse

Index of Photographs in and Around Chester

Shropshire Union Canal, Chester 4

The Gate Keeper Inn, Chester 4

Shropshire Union Canal Main Line, Chester 4

Frodsham Street Bridge over Shropshire Union Canal 4

Chester Cathedral Tower and Turrets 4

Frodsham Street, Chester Black and White Buildings 5

Frodsham Street, Chester Black and White Revival Architecture. 5

Frodsham Street, Chester Black and White Revival Architecture. 5

Frodsham Street, Chester Black and White Revival Architecture. 5

Frodsham Street, Chester Black and White Ornate Design 5

Frodsham Street, Chester 5

Frodsham Street, Chester Black and White Revival Architecture. 6

Black & White Revival Architecture St. Werburgh Street, Chester 6

Black & White Revival Architecture St. Werburgh Street, Chester 6

Black & White Revival Architecture St. Werburgh Street, Chester 6

Black & White Revival Architecture St. Werburgh Street, Chester 6

Black & White Revival Architecture 6

The Addleshaw Tower, Chester and City Walls 7

The Addleshaw Bell Tower, Chester - Front View 7

The Addleshaw Tower 7

Steps to City Walls by Chester's Cathedral 7

City Walls Walk by Chester's Cathedral 7

Bell Tower Walk, Chester 8

St. Werburgh Street, Chester Architecture 8
St. Werburgh Street, Chester Architecture 8
St. Werburgh Street, Chester..8
Chester Cathedral..8
Chester Cathedral Remembrance Garden to Cheshire Regiment
....8
Chester Cathedral 22nd Cheshire Regiment Memorial 9
Chester Cathedral 22nd Cheshire Regiment Memorial 9
Chester Cathedral with Cross Memorial 9
Chester Cathedral...9
Chester Cathedral...9
Chester Cathedral's view from the Garden of Remembrance 10
Winged Statue Chester Cathedral 10
Turret, Chester Cathedral 10
Chester Cathedral, Main Entrance..10
Janya 10
Chester Town Hall 10
East Gate Clock, Chester 11
East Gate Clock 11
East Gate Clock, Chester. 11
East Gate Street, Chester 1883 Architecture 11
The Chester Grosvenor 12
East Gate Street, Chester...12
Architecture East Gate Street, Chester......................................12
Temple Bar, Chester..12
Frodsham Street Architecture 12
Frodsham Street Architecture 13

Mill Hotel and Spa, with Canal Barge, Chester 13

Shropshire Union Canal Main Line, Chester 13

Steam Mill, Chester..................13

Chester City Walls from Canal..................13

North-East Tower Chester Walls, King Charles I Tower, Phoenix Tower, Newton Tower..................14

Broughton Water Tower, Chester 14

Chemistry Lock, Shropshire Union Canal, Chester 14

Chemistry Lock, Shropshire Union Canal, Chester 14

Sunset at Chemistry Lock, Cheshire..................14

After the rain, Chester Canal 15

Black and White Revival Architecture Chester 15

Black and White Revival Architecture Chester 15

Black and White Revival Architecture Chester 15

East Gate Street and East Gate Clock 15

East Gate Clock..................16

Black and White Revival Architecture..................16

Marlborough Arms, East Gate Street, Chester 16

Welsh Presbyterian Church, City Road, Chester..................16

Welsh Presbyterian Church, City Road, Chester..................17

East Gate Street Clock, Chester..................17

East Gate Street Clock, Chester..................17

Arch East Gate Street with Clock above..................17

East Gate Clock Ironwork 17

East Gate Small Archway 18

Owen Jones Died 1858 Stone Plaque 18

Colourful Shields Chester 18

The Chester Grosvenor, Hotel 18
East Gate Street, Black and White Buildings 18
Grosvenor Hotel Emblem, Chester 18
East Gate Street Black and White Buildings 19
Godstall Lane Sign 19
East Gate Street Architectural Building 19
East Gate Street Black and White Revival Architecture 19
East Gate Street Black and White Revival Architecture 19
East Gate and Clock, Street Level 20
East Gate Black and White Revival Buildings 20
Boot Inn, Established 1643, Chester 20
Black and White Revival Architecture 20
The Guild Church of St. Peter at the Cross, Chester 20
Corner of East Gate Street and Bridge Street, Revival Architecture 20
Chester Cross 21
Chester Lions Jubilee Bench adjacent to the Chester Cross 21
Bridge Street with Black and White Buildings 21
Black and White Revival Buildings 1888 21
Black and White Revival Buildings, Bridge Street, Chester 21
TC 1664 Black and White Buildings, Bridge Street, Chester 21
TC 1664 Black and White Buildings Detail, Bridge Street, Chester 22
Bridge Street, Black and White Buildings 22
Bridge Street, Black and White Buildings 22
Bridge Street, looking towards the Guild of St. Peter at the Cross Church 22
St. Peter at the Cross Church, Chester, Clock Tower 22

Grosvenor Shopping Centre, Chester 23
Dewa Roman Experience 23
Dewa Roman Experience Roman Tablet 23
Dewa Roman Experience Jail 23
Bridge Street Art Gallery, Chester 23
Bridge Street, Modern Black and White Architecture 24
St. Michael's Church, Chester, History & Heritage Centre 24
Grosvenor Street, Chester 24
The Saddle Inn, Chester 24
Grosvenor Museum Chester 1886 24
Grosvenor Museum, Exterior Architecture 25
Grosvenor Museum Exterior Architecture, Chester 25
Cenotaph to Matthew Henry, Chester 25
Grosvenor Museum, Chester 25
Matthew Henry Obelisk 25
Grosvenor Museum Clock, Chester 25
Tower, Chester Castle 26
Field Marshal Stapleton Cotton, 1st Viscount Combermere GCB, GCH, KSI, PC Equestrian Statue 26
Chester's Military Museum 26
Mathew Henry Obelisk, on roundabout near Grosvenor Museum, Chester 26
Clock Tower and Chimneys of the Grosvenor Museum, Chester 26
Cheshire Military Museum 26
The Propylaeum, Chester Castle 27
Winged Dragon, Cheshire Military Museum 27

St. Mary's Church, Tower, Chester behind the University of Chester's entrance 27

Queen Victoria Statue Chester Castle 27

Queen Victoria's Statue Embellishments and Crests, Chester's Castle 27

The 22nd Cheshire Regiment, Plaque, Queen Victoria's Statue Chester Castle 27

Chester's Crown Court situated next to Chester's Castle. 28

Statue of Field Marshall Stapleton Cotton through the Propylaeum, from the Statue of Queen Victoria 28

Cheshire County Council Hundredth Centenary Plaque 28

Chester Castle Entrance 28

Queen Victoria's Statue from the rear 28

Archway to Chester's Castle 28

Chester's Tower and Castle 29

Fortified Prison Door, Chester Castle 29

Portico, Chester Castle and Crown Courts 29

Forecourt, Chester's Castle and Crown Court with Queen Victoria's Statue 29

Portico Chester's Castle 30

University of Chester Entrance 30

St. Mary's Church Tower, Chester 30

Architecture opposite St. Mary's Church, Chester 30

St Mary's Church Gates, Chester 31

St. Mary's Church Front, Chester 31

St. Mary's Church, Tower Details 31

St. Mary's Church Millennium Festive Trail Plaque 2000 31

Architecture, Chester 31

Grosvenor 1886 Museum Plaque 31
Catholic Church, St. Francis of Assisi 32
Foundation Stone, Grosvenor Museum 32
Grosvenor Museum, Entrance Staircase 32
Grosvenor Museum, Mosaic on Staircase 32
Chester Castle Walls 32
Chester Castle Exterior Profile 32
Castle Drive Bridge, Chester Castle 33
Chester's Castle Fortifications and Walls 33
Castle Drive Bridge 33
Grosvenor Bridge Model, Chester 33
Grosvenor Bridge, Chester 33
City Wall and Chester Castle 33
City Walls, Chester 34
River Dee, by Handbridge 34
Rock Formation by River Dee 34
Trees along the River Dee 34
University of Chester 34
Handbridge, Chester 34
Handbridge, Chester and River Dee 35
Handbridge, Chester Windows Architecture 35
Handbridge Chester, Arches 35
The Bridgegate, Chester 35
Chester Weir 35
View of the Groves, from Handbridge 35
River Dee at Chester Weir 36
Handbridge Building 36

Chester Weir and River Dee 36
City Walls along River Dee 36
River Dee, Chester Weir 36
River Boats, Chester's River Dee 36
Waterfall by Handbridge, Chester 37
River Dee looking towards University of Chester 37
Handbridge Road Architecture 37
Minerva's Shrine, Chester, Edgar's Field 37
Rock Formation below Minerva's Shrine 37
Handbridge, Chester from Edgar's Field 37
University of Chester 38
River Dee and Handbridge, Chester 38
River Dee and Handbridge 38
Handbridge 38
Handbridge Arch 38
Plaque Norman Weir 38
Prince of Wales' Feathers Plaque 39
Bear and Billet Pub, Lower Bridge Street, Chester 39
Bridgegate, Chester 39
Plaque, Bridgegate, Chester 39
The Bridgegate 39
Edgar House, Chester 40
Handbridge Chester Arches 40
Trees on the embankment of the River Dee 40
The Bandstand by the River Dee and the Groves 40
Bandstand by the River Dee and the Groves 40
River Dee and Handbridge 41

Queen's Park Suspension Bridge, Chester 41
Queen's Park Suspension Bridge City of Chester, 1923 41
Chester Architecture 41
City of Chester Plaque 41
The Groves and Bandstand, Chester 41
River Dee at Chester 42
"Welcome To Queen's Park 1923" Signage 42
River Dee from Queen's Park, Chester 42
Queen's Park Suspension Bridge Span.................................... 42
Welcome to the Groves 2012 Plaque 42
Queen's Park Suspension Bridge Arch.................................... 43
Grosvenor Park, Quarry and Arches from St. Michael's Church, West Door 43
Arch from West Door of Old St. Michael's Church 43
Grosvenor Park Quarry and Arches – Jacob's well and St. Mary's Nunnery Arches 43
Arch from West Door of Old St. Michael's Church 44
Jacob's Well Arch, Grosvenor Park 44
St. Mary's Nunnery Three Arches, Grosvenor Park.................. 44
St. Mary's Nunnery Arches Rear View..................................... 44
The Old Shipgate Arch, Grosvenor Park, Chester.................... 44
Richard Grosvenor, Stone Statue 44
610 Squadron Memorial... 45
Grosvenor Park Pond, Chester.. 45
Grosvenor Park Pond, Chester.. 45
Black & White Modern Architecture 45
St. Werburgh Church, Chester... 45

Training Pavilion, Grosvenor Park 46
The Family, Grosvenor Park, Chester 46
The Family is a nation in miniature 46
The Church of St. John the Baptist Ruins..................................46
Belfry and Clock Tower, St John's the Baptist Church, Chester.46
The Church of St. John the Baptist Ruins..................................46
The Corner Stone, St. John the Baptist Church 47
Belfry and Clock Tower, St. John the Baptist Church, Chester ..47
St. John the Baptist Church, Chester - side view......................47
St. John's Church, Millennium Festival Trail Plaque 2000..........47
St. John's Church Arched Entrance..47
St. John the Baptist Church, Approach, Chester 48
Roman Amphitheatre, Chester 48
The Newgate, Chester...48
Roman Gardens Mosaic Chester Civil Trust MMX 48
Roman Gardens, Chester..48
Black and White Buildings, Park Street, Chester.......................48
Black and White Architecture, Park Street, Chester 49
Newgate Bridge, Chester, Steps to City Wall 49
Spire, Chester..49
Turret building, Pepper Street, Chester 49
Pepper Street, Chapel, Chester...50
Pepper Street, Chapel, Chester Plaque 50
St. Michael's Church, Chester 50
Black & White Revival Architecture...50
Chester Cross & Bridge Street..50
Black & White Revival Architecture, Northgate Street, Chester..51

The Town Hall, Chester 51

A Celebration of Chester Statue, Northgate Street 51

Millennium Festival Trail Town Hall 2000 Plaque 51

Stone Carving, "Hugh Lupus, Created Earl of Chester" 52

Stone Carvings and Doors, Town Hall, Chester 52

Cheshire County Council Roll of Honour the Great War 1914 - 1918 52

Staircase, Town Hall, Chester 52

Arches and Stained Glass Windows, Town Hall Chester 53

Wall Shields, Town Hall, Chester 53

"*James the Second Welcomed by the Citizens and Nobility*", Stone Sculpture, Town Hall 53

"*Edward Prince of Wales Receiving Homage, First Royal Earl of Chester A.D. 1254*" 53

"*Charter Granted to Mayor and Corporation by Randolph the Third A.D. 1181*", *Stone Sculpture, Town Hall* 53

Ornate Chairs and Windows, Town Hall, Chester 53

Wooden Balcony, Town Hall, Chester 54

Ornate Fireplace, Town Hall, Chester 54

Wooden Balcony and Clock Face and Inscription, Town Hall 54

Staircase, looking upward, Town Hall, Chester 54

"*The Entry of Charles the First into Chester*", Stone Sculpture, Town Hall 54

Roman Soldiers Building the Walls of Chester, Stone Sculpture Town Hall 55

Water Fountain, Chester Cathedral 55

View from Cloister Garth, Chester Cathedral 55

North Tower, Chester Cathedral 55

Cloister Garth, with Fountain of Life, Chester Cathedral 55

North Tower from Cloister Garth, Chester Cathedral...................56

Cloisters, Chester Cathedral..56

Cloister Garth, with Fountain of Life, Chester Cathedral 56

Cross and North Tower, Chester Cathedral................................56

North Tower, Chester Cathedral..56

Altar Engravings, Chester Cathedral 57

Millennium Festival Trail 2000, East Gate Clock Plaque 57

Canal Side, City of Chester..57

River Dee..57

The Old Dee Bridge, Handbridge..57

About Felicity McCullough

Felicity McCullough has been taking photographs for many years and she has decided to publish some of her photographs in bite-size glimpses and this is her next glimpse in the series "Places to Visit".

Newton Abbot A Photographic Glimpse

Additionally, she has written several books about preventative health care for goats. The website dedicated to goats www.goatlapshop.com has a wide variety of topics and resources that relate to goats, including other guides in the Goat Knowledge Series and the Charlie And Isabella's Magical Adventures Series of Children's Books, suitable for bed-time reading that are beautifully illustrated.

Index

CHESTER	1
A PHOTOGRAPHIC GLIMPSE	1
Copyright	2
Introduction to this Photographic Glimpse of Chester	3
Additional Chester Information	58
Addleshaw Tower	58
Architecture Chester	58
Bandstand by the River Dee and the Groves;	59
Bear and Billett Public House	59
Bell Tower Walk, Chester	59
Boot Inn, Chester	59
Bridge Street	59
Bridgegate, Chester	60
Broughton Water Tower, Chester	60
'Celebration of Chester' Statue	60
Chester Canal	61
Chester Castle	61
Chester Cathedral	62
Chester City Walls	63
Chester Cross	63
Chester's Crown Court	63
Chester Grosvenor Hotel	64
Chester Lions	64
Chester Weir	64
Cheshire County Council	64

Chester Town Hall	65
Cheshire Regiment	66
Cotton, Field Marshal Stapleton, 1st Viscount Combermere GCB, GCH, KSI, PC	67
Dewa Roman Experience	67
East Gate	67
East Gate Street, Chester	69
Edgar's Field	69
Edgar House, Chester	69
Frodsham Street, Chester	69
Godstall Lane	69
Grosvenor	69
Groves	71
Guild Church of St Peter at the Cross, Chester	71
Handbridge, Chester	72
History and Heritage	72
Jacob's Well, Grosvenor Park, Chester	72
Janya	73
Lock Keeper Inn, Chester	73
Map of Chester	73
Marlborough Arms	73
Matthew Henry VDM Cenotaph	73
Millennium Festival Trail, Chester	74
[Mill Hotel & Spa Website](#)	74
Military Museum	74
Minerva's Shrine, Chester	74
Newgate Chester	75

North East Tower, City Walls Chester	75
Northgate Street, Chester	75
Owen Jones	75
Pepper Street	75
Prince of Wales' Feathers	76
Queen's Park	76
Queen Victoria's Statue	76
Richard Grosvenor, 2nd Marquis of Westminster	77
River Dee	78
Rock Formation	78
Roman Amphitheatre, Chester	78
Roman Gardens	79
Saddle Inn, Chester	79
Shields	79
Shipgate Arch, Grosvenor Park, Chester	79
St. Francis of Assisi	79
St. John's the Baptist Church, Chester	79
St. Mary's Church, Chester	80
St. Mary's Nunnery	80
St. Michael's Church, Chester	81
St. Peter at the Cross Church, Chester	81
St. Werburgh Church, Chester	82
St. Werburgh Street, Chester	82
Steam Mill, Chester	82
Temple Bar	82
Town Hall, Chester	82
University of Chester	84

Welsh Presbyterian Church, Chester	84
610 Squadron	84
Index of Photographs in and Around Chester	86
About [Felicity McCullough](#)	98
Index	99
Publisher	103

Publisher

[My Lap Shop Publishers](#)
91 Mayflower Street, Unit 222,
Plymouth, Devon, PL1 1SB
United Kingdom
Tel: +44 (0)871 560 5297
www.mylapshop.com
[About My Lap Shop Publishers](#)

First Edition March 2014